KID WITHOUT FEAR

I shiver when I think of how crazy we were – all of us were eight to ten years old. It was great entertainment that we designed and staged ourselves. If one of those shells had ever tipped in our direction, we could have been fried or could have watched the house burn down. Let's face it – we were lucky to have survived these escapades.

Some might ask – where were your parents? They must have been either at work or out on the pastures guarding the farm animals. For the most part, children were left to pursue their own entertainment, dangerous as it was.

In Budapest, most everything was rationed and usually out of stock. Many stores had nothing in them, the shelves were bare. I spent countless hours standing in line in the early hours of the morning – sometimes as early as 2am – just for meagre portions of bread, sugar or meat. My shoes were worn out. I had no winter clothes. Sometimes I almost froze to death while waiting in line. It was next to impossible to find fruits or vegetables. It was tremendously upsetting when the store ran out of a product just before I got to the door; and unfortunately this happened a lot.

Behind the schools and the factory, there was a huge vacant lot with hundreds of T-34 Russian tanks. The Russians put up a fence and a gate on the tracks and kept the wagons on the incline away from the school. We were not allowed to walk through the field of tanks anymore, and we couldn't play with the railroad cars either. They posted sentries to walk the property, and they caught me once with some useless tank part. I was scared to death when I was made to kneel in front of the captain's office. Mostly I was upset that I had been caught. The sentry pointed a machine pistol at my back, and although I knew he wasn't going to shoot me – he was just trying to scare me – I promised I would never enter the property again and I never did.

Kid Without Fear

Charles Eric Jambor

Kid Without Fear

Autobiography and Memoir of

Charles Eric Jambor

KAROLY-J
LTD.
Publishing

Publishers Note: This work is the autobiography and memoir of Charles Eric Jambor. All individuals and events have been recorded as seen and experienced through the personal life of Charles Eric Jambor.

"Kid Without Fear" can be ordered by e-mailing Charles Eric Jambor, directly: yardmarx@nornet.on.ca It is also available on Amazon.

Published by Karoly-J Ltd. Publishing

Library and Archives Canada Cataloguing in Publication

Jambor, Charles E. (Charles Eric), author
Kid Without Fear / Charles Eric Jambor

Issued in print and electronic format
ISBN 978-0-9940881-0-9(ppk.) – ISBN 13: 978-
0994088109/10:0994088108

1.   Jambor, Charles E. (Charles Eric). 2. Engineers – Ontario –
Biography. 3. Hungarian Canadians – Ontario – Biography.
4. Inventors – Ontario– Biography. 5. World War, 1939-1945
– Hungary. I. Title.

Dedicated To

My Parents,
Who worked so hard for so little.

Charles Eric Jambor

Acknowledgements

In memory of Johnny Onodi, my cousin, who is long gone. He had everything to do with my survival. I was only eight years old during WWII. He taught me all I needed to know in those days, including how to diffuse landmines. Thank you Johnny.

Some of his grandchildren and other family members are still living, and I am certain they will read this book. Special thanks to Douglas Lintula for helping me with the arrangement of my early memoirs when my book was called "I Shouldn't Be Here". Thanks also to Cavern of Dreams.

To my children, Bobbi and Carrie, who contributed greatly offering many helpful suggestions. Most importantly, to Erika, my wife, who helped with the tedious task of editing.

There are two friends, Keith Ashley and Al Eizinas who have read my story and encouraged me to continue. Also many thanks to Terry Davis at Ball Media, for designing a great cover for "Kid Without Fear".

Charles Eric Jambor

Prologue

Being in the centre of Europe, Hungary was always at the crossroads of not only travellers, but dictators, invaders and occupiers as well. The 20th century saw them all. At the beginning of World War II, Hungary was neutral for a short period, enjoying relative peace within its borders. That all changed when Germany attacked the Soviet Union in 1941 and forced Miklos Horthy, head of the Hungarian government, to declare war on the allies.

But the war didn't go well for the Germans, and the Russian army advanced through Europe. By April 4, 1945, the Germans were pushed out of Hungary. Hungary's regime changed from Nazism to communism. The following years saw more controls forced onto Hungary until tensions came to head in October of 1956, and an armed uprising began against the Russians.

Hungary's heroic efforts were crushed quickly by Russian tanks, and indiscriminate shelling again heavily damaged Budapest. Over ten thousand perished and thousands of young people were arrested. For a couple of months, the border to the west was left open and many escaped to Austria. After the Austrian border closed, others – including myself – fled to the south, to Yugoslavia, a country with a different style of communism, but one that allowed me to make my way to Canada: the land of the free, the land of opportunity.

This is my story...

Charles Eric Jambor

Part One

Charles Eric Jambor

Hungary

Chapter one

I stare at my picture on the wall and wonder how many of us can say "I made it".

~

"That vineyard up on the hill had to be the most peaceful place on earth. I cherished the nights when Johnny and I laid on our backs in a haystack looking at the million stars above. He would tell me stories about the universe, the constellations - the Big Dipper and the Little Dipper while the crickets chirped and a wolf howled behind the vineyard in the forest. I am misty-eyed as I write this.

Johnny taught me how to harness horses and hook them up to a wagon. He taught me how to make a windmill with June-bugs and how to chop down a tree with an axe. He taught me how to cut clover with a sickle and many other things we don't even do any more now a days. He showed me how to make a whistle from a willow twig. It was a meticulous job and you had to do it just right. I think I could still make one today. He was my best buddy in those days. I would listen to his fascinating stories until I fell asleep".
But let's go back; to the beginning.

hile to me my birth was incidental, to my mom it was a

major event. I was born by C-section. Luckily I saw daylight in a developed country and in a city that had hospitals and doctors who knew how to handle a difficult birth. I was born in Budapest, Hungary on March 26, 1936.

What I have written here is real and is verifiable. However sometimes I brag a little and joke when I should be serious and am serious when I should be joking. As to my parents, I just wish they were around to read this autobiography and memoir.

I didn't intentionally dig into my parent's lives or their intimate relationships but through their conversations with relatives and friends I learned a lot of interesting things about them.

I knew we had relatives in Budapest, in Simontornya, and in Nemedi but I certainly didn't know about relatives in another country.

I found out later that we even had relatives in the USA in Florida and in Ohio. The latter was a real surprise and joy.

~

My parents, Rose (Rozalia) & Karoly, Wedding Day – 1933

Allegedly I was a bad baby. I didn't want to go to sleep. I cried all night and most of the day. I usually screamed the loudest when my dad came home from the night shift. I credit my mom for saving me because I remember hearing my dad joke in a number of conversations with friends and family that had it been up to him he might have thrown me out into the yard or given me away.

I have no idea why I cried so much, but possibly I had colic. My crankiness couldn't even be blamed on any food because all I was getting was mother's milk. But despite my crankiness, I was loved. I know that when I cried, my mom picked me up and cuddled me. I must have been crying for reasons other than wanting attention because I got all the attention in the world; it must have been colic.

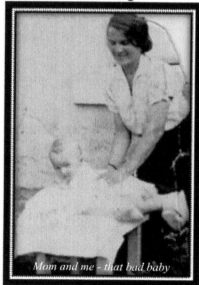

Mom and me - that bad baby

~

My own earliest recollections began when I was in Kindergarten. I started having dreams as soon as I was sent to bed. I imagined tiny, furry animals, like opossums, putting me on their backs. They would take me under the bed, in front of it, and around it, several times until I finally fell into a deep sleep. These little animals never hurt me but this was a recurring dream that I experienced for some time. Possibly this strange dream started when my parents wanted me to go to bed and would say; "The *poccis* are coming to get you, if you don't go to sleep…" (pronounced pokkies) As far as I know there were no such animals in Hungary or in any other country. I think parents often made up these imaginary creatures to prompt their children into behaving. Perhaps these *pokkies* were created by my mom or dad, I will never know for sure.

Around the same time my dad was a porcelain decorator at a dinner ware factory called Keramia in Kispest and used to bring home faulty decals, I was told. I plastered them all over walls and windows. He would come home covered in white dust looking like a ghost. The decals didn't stick too well so my mom was able to remove them easily.

~

Overall I think I was a pretty normal child. I had curly blond hair, a cute round face and had a happy disposition, which I have retained to this day.

When I grew out of diapers my mom gave me more freedom and I was quite active and managed to get myself into just about everything!

Charles at the age of two years

Chapter Two

My mom gives away our cat – the cat came back. But then leaves us anyway. I learn the Morse code. I attempt a stunt with a broken collarbone. My landlady tries to poison me.

The first house I remember living in was a detached one bedroom house at 142 Nagy Sandor Street, in Kispest which is a suburb of Budapest. It had no insulation with only plaster on the walls. You can imagine how cold it was in the winter. This house was located on the right side of a large lot, while the main building, the landlord's house was on the left. The buildings are still there today. I went to visit our old house in 2003. The person living there (I believe was already the tenth owner of the place) wouldn't allow me into the yard thinking I had some sort of a claim on the property. I told him I had not lived in Hungary for the past fifty years so he had nothing to worry about.

The house we used to live in had a shed and an outhouse attached to it and it backed onto the next-door neighbour's building. I recall my dad being woken up at night by terrible noises, and with water hose in hand he would chase yowling cats off the roof. The cats must have been in heat because they made one heck of a racket!

Once, the next-door neighbour had the same idea as my dad and at the same time. In the middle of the night the two of them sprayed each other across the roof! I remember my dad telling the tale many times and every time I heard it I found it funnier than the time before. My imagination made it wilder and wilder and I find it funny even today; in fact, I believe I could write a whole story on just that one incident.

My dad had to be in his mid-twenties. I imagine that he was probably not wearing much more than his underwear as he paraded in the yard in front of the landlady and her husband, who had also been awakened by the cats. In some countries, I suppose he could have been charged with indecent exposure. Thank goodness this was not the case here!

~

The kitchen in our house had a tiled floor and my mom used to put down a pillow for me to sit on. I used to take apart wooden jam boxes and saved the little nails. I straightened them when they were crooked and used them over and over again to make little houses and stools from the slats. My dad showed me how to hold the nails to avoid hitting my fingers. I was good at creating items out of wood, a skill I retain even today.

I also made a ramp for a little tank I had received for Christmas one year. It was a wind-up, camouflaged German Tiger tank. It had knobby rubber crawlers and a white cross painted on both sides. I built the ramp steeper and steeper until my tank couldn't climb it anymore. I over-wound it once and took it apart to fix it, but neither I nor my mom could put it back together again.

Today, most people wouldn't even bother to try and fix a toy; they'd just throw it out and buy a new one.

~

My dad was conscripted into the army when I was about four years old. Miraculously he returned after his tour of service, about a year later. He was with the communications unit and taught me the Morse code, which I remembered for years. Now, I have forgotten most of the codes because I never had to use them. All I can recall today is SOS (...---...). It was cool though. Not many kids in my kindergarten class knew it and sometimes I would brag to show off my special knowledge.

The *Enigma* machine, a more sophisticated method of sending messages took the place of Morse code towards the end of the war. I wasn't too happy because now no one paid attention to my Morse signals. I even went to my teacher to complain that nobody would answer my Morse code. She just laughed and told me to go use the phone.

~

I used to play with our cat. I wasn't very gentle with it. I would pick it up by its neck or tail and set it up on my shoulder. She must have been a mellow creature because she didn't care and I don't remember her ever scratching me. One time though, my dad scolded me for knocking over his ironed shirts with the cat.

My mom decided to give the cat to my grandparents who lived in the country. Likely, the horrible yowling noises at night had a lot to do with her decision. Neutering was rarely heard of and most families couldn't afford it anyway. Mom put the cat in a cane basket, and we travelled by train to my grandparent's place. With the train stopping at every station it was a long ride. The cat meowed all the way.

I missed my cat every day and was overjoyed when three months or so later, she found her way back to us! We were amazed to see her again. To return home she would have had to cross several creeks and the Danube River. She was scruffy and hungry, but otherwise no worse for wear. My parents talked a lot about her incredible feat.

Unfortunately a couple of years later she suffocated in the oven of our wood stove. To conserve heat my dad had closed the oven door that she used to sit on. One time she curled up deep inside the oven to keep warm and nobody noticed. I remember seeing her stiff as a stuffed toy, crouched down on her front legs. We all cried. She had been a very nice cat.

~

Our landlord, Balatoni Bacsi was an elderly gentleman - a tall, thick-set, kind-looking man with a heart of gold. Mrs. Balatoni wasn't as nice. I don't think she liked me. Maybe it had something to do with the fact that I screamed so much as a baby, but even after I grew older, she didn't bother with me.

Before Mr. Balatoni retired, he worked for the *Magyar Allami Vasut* (Hungarian National Railway). Working on the trains gave him the opportunity to travel all over Europe. He and my dad would often talk for hours about the exciting adventures Mr. Balatoni had on company expense. My dad became excited about having that kind of a job and eventually decided to join the railroad after his service in the army. He had no idea though, what he was getting into. To work on a train engine during the war was equal to suicide; the first thing to get knocked out was the locomotive. There were also the blown up bridges and railroad tracks to worry about, as well as collisions with other trains. It often happened that two trains would be bombed at the same time as they passed each other on the tracks. How he managed to survive we will never know. Like me, my father was lucky.

~

During the years we lived there, Mrs. Balatoni would sometimes invite me over for a snack or a bowl of soup. One day after I ate some split pea soup, my stomach swelled up like a huge balloon; even my mom's nightgown wouldn't fit me. My dad rolled me up in a blanket, put me in a wheelbarrow and rushed me to the hospital. The doctor said I'd had an allergic reaction to the dried yellow peas in the soup. He gave me an injection and I was better the next day.

Mrs. Balatoni never fed me dried peas again. She was truly sorry for what had happened and from then on, she was nice to me. My parents didn't blame her and knew it wasn't intentional. Years later I ate lots of split peas of all colours and none of them gave me a problem. In fact I love split pea soup.

~

I used to play with Mr. Balatoni's nephew, Gabi when he came to visit. He was about three years older than me and at that time, he was the most interesting, clever person in the world. He always had nifty ideas, things he probably dreamed up the day before and then shared them with me, perhaps because I was so receptive to his ideas. I enjoyed having him as a teacher. Sometimes he would bring me toys that he had made.

One day he decided to make a little well using a large can. He buried it in the ground and then took a smaller can and used it as a pail. Using strings he lowered the small can into the *well*, but it didn't want to tilt. He attached a little pebble to one side of the can and then it tilted. We could draw water from it.

Gabi showed me how to make pretend cars, trucks and tanks out of broken pieces of wood. I was eager to learn. Together we built roads in the sand. We made little rivers with the well water and drove our vehicles right through them. They didn't get stuck because they didn't have any wheels; we were the engines that propelled them. We played on those roads for hours, until we tired.

In those days most toys were made in Germany and they were expensive. We were not well off and my parents couldn't afford to buy me new toys. I was lucky I guess to have had a friend like Gabi to share adventures with and learn from.

~

Mr. Balatoni had a beautiful garden full of the most wonderful flowers, including the prettiest dahlias I have ever seen in my life. He also had a turtle that he kept for years. It was around ten centimetres in diameter. He said the turtle was beneficial for the garden because it caught all the bugs. In the winter he would put the turtle in a pail of wheat mash and keep the pail in the shed. He also raised rabbits for food. I remember they didn't need any water to drink, but they smelled really bad. That stench stayed in my nose forever.

Milike and I

The Balatonis also had a beautiful Phillips radio in their kitchen that I used to admire and listen to when I had a chance.

I thought about owning one someday myself.

Mr Balatoni had two teenagers from his first marriage. Amelia was sixteen and her brother Dodi was fifteen. Amelia was drop dead gorgeous. She used to babysit me sometimes when my mother had to work or go to the market. She seemed to adore me and frankly, the feeling was mutual.

Dodi wanted to be a mechanical engineer. He told me I should become one too, when I grew up. I took his advice and have never regretted it. He joined the Arrow Cross Youth Organization, the youth faction of the Arrow Cross Party. Dodi used to come home with his .22 calibre rifle resting on his shoulder. I can still picture him today walking down the street in his brown uniform with a swagger to his step. He looked really cool. I envied him and wanted to grow up and look just like him.

The last time I saw Dodi he was around eighty years old and living in Torrance, California. Sadly, he looked unwell and I felt sorry for him. He had previously lived in Brazil with his American wife who had been the secretary to a US attaché. They had moved around the world a lot. When I visited Dodi in Torrance I felt like I was entering an antique shop. There were vases, statues, expensive paintings, chairs, sofas, rolled-up carpets and about two dozen unopened boxes scattered all over the house. He told me in broken English and Hungarian that his wife had died a few years before.

He gave me a large ceramic plate and another one to take to his sister. The plates were from the Orient and they looked expensive. He talked about a weird religion that he and his late wife had practised and tried to convert me. I didn't want to break his heart so I converted for the day. I left his house with a heavy heart and promised to call him. I did, many times but no one answered the phone. When I contacted the Los Angeles police, they said there had been a death in that house.

~

Mr. Balatoni's property on Nagy Sandor St. was the second one from the end of the street. It had a two metre high picket fence around it. On the opposite side of this property there was a convenience store that sold candies, shoelace liquorice, foaming crystal sugar and pickled herring in a barrel. To this day I can taste the delicacy of that herring in my mouth. The store owners were an older Jewish couple. The vision of them being marched away with the yellow Star of David pinned to their overcoats is still vivid in my memory. I remember they looked at me and I looked back. That was the last time I ever saw them. I don't know what happened to them or their store after they were taken away.

~

The street was always dusty because it was a dirt road. It had a shallow ditch on either side which was overgrown with grass and weeds. At the street corner the ditch on our side had a flattened-out metal culvert that housed a family of hedge dogs. They were very cute. Hedge dogs have narrower faces than their cousins the hedgehogs. I used to pick them up and pet them. They seemed to like that because they made a murmuring sound, similar to a cat. I remember taking two of them into the house and feeding them milk.

The ditch on our side of the street is hugely significant to me because when I was about five years old, I tripped into it and broke my left collarbone. I remember being in the hospital for the longest time with my arm in a cast, elevated at 90 degrees to my body. It must have been in the middle of summer because the cherries were ripening on a tree in the hospital's yard. Those cherries didn't seem to be too high up so without

Ditch where I broke my collarbone

fear, I pulled a wagon close to the tree, and climbed on it. But even by standing on the wagon I couldn't reach the cherries. I went and got a garden table and a chair and stacked them onto the wagon. I don't know whether I was on the table yet or not, but I was definitely reaching for that enticing fruit when my doctor came by and asked me what on earth I thought I was doing. Luckily he didn't raise his voice or he would have scared me and I would have fallen.

This incident became legendary in our family, and as I found out later, in the doctor's family as well. I remember my parents talking about this often. It isn't something I would advise anyone to do; with or without a broken collarbone.

~

As I remember in the 1940s our favorite relative, Yany *(Jani bacsi)* who was my Aunt Julia's only son would visit. Julia was married to a man whose family name was Szing (pronounced Sing but not East Indian) who apparently died in WWI. Yany was two or three years older than my dad. During one of his visits I was playing doctor with a little girl likely the same age I was, when Yany found us under the steps to the attic. Even though I had hung a tarp over the entrance to our hideaway, we were discovered. I was the doctor and she was the patient. She had all her clothes off and I don't remember whether I had mine off or not. I am certain nothing *perverse* had taken place. Yany though, was laughing and said; "he's starting pretty early!" Of course at the time I had no idea what he meant.

Chapter Three

I break my collarbone again. I soil my pants. The Germans invade Hungary but the kids befriend the soldiers. (Personal note; kids should be running the world). I become semi fluent in German. My first major incident happens. A gander gooses me. Our landlord builds a 'bomb shelter'.

In the summer of 1942, I slipped on a stone and broke my other collarbone in the same ditch and almost at the same exact spot. I was lucky that school hadn't started yet. By the time it did, the cast was off and I could attend my first grade.

The teacher was a lovely lady, but she was tough. Only a few weeks into the school year I remember that I had needed to go to the bathroom. I had put my hand up and had asked to be excused but she told me to wait for the recess buzzer. I tried and tried but I couldn't hold it and soiled my pants. The kid sitting behind me noticed the smell and reported me to the teacher and she sent me home.

When I got to my house I climbed up the gate and rang the bell. Gates were always kept locked on all fences in Hungary and across central Europe. Anyone wanting to visit us had to pull on a long wire that was connected to the bell.

My mom was surprised to see me home that early in the day but once I told her what had happened she didn't blame me. She was angry with the teacher though. I have often wondered about such rules. How can a six-year-old be expected to hold back a bowel movement for any length of time?

That same year on a day trip into the forest with my

class I was scolded for pulling a leaf off a tree. Never mind the million bombs that fell all over the world during the war destroying thousands of buildings and countless trees; we were supposed to respect Nature.

~

A week or two after school started we visited my father's brother Joe, in Erd near Budapest. At that time it was a new development and there were only a few buildings on the street. Not far from my uncle's house there was a cave that a lot of people came to visit. The cave had bats in it and even though my mom and I were afraid to go in we went in anyway. I admired the stalactites and gaping holes - they were awesome.

When we came out of the cave there was a gaggle of geese grazing close by and my dad had warned me not to go near them. I tried not to but I guess I was closer than I thought because a gander attacked me! It pinched my behind with its beak causing me to scream. I was wearing shorts that day and was lucky the goose didn't pinch my bare legs. Fortunately my dad rescued me. I learned a good lesson that day - always keep a good distance between me and a goose.

~

In the fall of that year the Germans occupied Hungary. A bunch of us kids watched as the soldiers filled our streets with tanks and other heavy vehicles. They took over the high school and a nearby park. I remember learning some German words like *Bitteschoen Zucker* (may I have some candies) as we climbed fearlessly all over their tanks.

~

The next year around the middle of August, we went on a day trip to Hungary's biggest body of water, Lake Balaton. The train stopped at Balatonederics, and from there we hoofed it a couple of kilometres to the beach. We walked two-by-two like soldiers but we certainly didn't behave like well-disciplined soldiers! In fact we were bad, horsing around all the way.

Like some of the other kids I started picking the soft tar out of the road's concrete expansion joints and was using it to form a walnut-sized ball which I mounted on a stick. I made the handle long enough to get a good grip on it. While I was being clobbered from behind I was clobbering kids ahead of me to the point that some started screaming. Even though almost everyone was involved in this ruckus, and the teacher didn't actually see *me* doing anything; I ended up catching the blame for bullying my schoolmates.

I was glad when we finally reached the lake, but here is where my first *major* death-defeating event took place. It all started when another boy and I found a small rowboat and decided to explore the lake on our own. We soon found ourselves stuck in a thick patch of canes and reeds. As we tried to free the boat we upset it instead. The next thing I remember was someone holding me by my feet and I was puking water. I almost drowned. The other boy had somehow scrambled to safety. My teacher thought I was a goner.

No one from the school told my parents about my misadventure. Had my mom found out what happened that day she would have taken a fit. She would never have let me go on such a trip again.

~

I could hardly wait to go to the amusement parks. There were two in Budapest. The one closest to us was called the Peoples' Park (*Népliget*) which was the biggest park. The one downtown was called the City Park (*Városliget*). The City Park had an ancient castle which everyone simply called 'The Castle.' It also had a lake, a mote and a bridge that lead to a classy public swimming pool (*Szécsenyi*). It had a winding road used for motorcycle races in the summer. My favourite motorbike was the Moto Guzzi. In the winter they used the lake for public skating.

I loved the Giant Wheel, the Merry-Go-Round and the Dodgem. There was no admission fee to the parks and the rides cost next to nothing. Usually I would go with my parents, a relative, or friends of the family.

The Peoples' Park had the same amenities as the City Park but it was in a forested area. My mom used to take a packed lunch and a blanket when we went there. I will never forget the music that came from the park. It was about a baby duck and it was a catchy little tune. Those were my happy days.

~

In the fall of 1943 when the allies began their assault on Budapest, my happy days ended. Precautionary measures had to be taken. Our landlord Mr. Balatoni had to sacrifice a good part of his beautiful garden to make a bomb shelter. I recall it wouldn't have sheltered us from a medium-sized pumpkin falling on its roof. He dug that shelter after a bomb exploded two streets over killing a family. The blast from that bomb broke our bedroom window. I still have a shard in my bum from that explosion.

Every time the air raid siren went off (which was five or six times a day) we, and some neighbours hurried to get into Mr. Balatoni's shelter. At night we had to cover our windows with sheets of blue paper so that no light showed through. That was of course, when we still had electricity. When the power went out the sirens stopped blowing and the bombs rained down on us day and night and we were forced to evacuate the city. My mom and I went to my grandparent's house in the country. This was the place we had taken our cat to. The same cat that found its way back to us in Budapest. If I remember correctly my dad had to stay behind in the city as he still had to work. Our evacuation was a non-issue to me. I do not remember being scared, excited or confused. To me it was just a war.

My dad thought we would be safer at my grandparents' place where we had been many times before. However, the opposite was true. There was war around us everywhere. To me though it was like a game. Children just want to eat, to play and to have their parents around. They will occupy themselves with anything and can cope just fine, even through a war.

Chapter Four

Grandfather Onodi's vineyard is where I first saw a cow, a horse and a blind dog. It's where I learned about machinery. It's where my cousins Juliska, Johnny and Mariska grew up.

Three generations lived at this vineyard. The Onodi's were my mother's parents. Their son Janos (my mom's brother) was married to Julia and they had three children – Juliska, Johnny and Mariska. Life was different here.

Whenever we visited the Onodi's, my mom and I would arrive by train during the night. When the train stopped in Simontornya we would get off not far from an artesian well where I'd always take a swig of the water even though I knew it would taste awful. It was hot and it smelled like sulphur or rotten eggs. I was fascinated by the way it came pouring out of a pipe always hot, even in the winter. We would walk from the station along the tracks and over a wooden trestle that spanned the Sió Canal (*Sió-csatoyrna*) out onto a crushed stone road which is now paved. We would walk by an enclosure housing a small statue of the Virgin Mary where my mom would always cross herself. Two kilometres past that Virgin Mary we would come to a row of houses and we would start walking on a dirt road and go all the way up the hill to my grandparents which was about another two kilometres.

After the war I remember filling up a tank trap in the area of that Virgin Mary statue. We buried thousands of shells, wrecked machinery, horses and maybe even some dead soldiers. Many people, including children, worked on that project for several days.

In the past when I was little and we were going for a visit, I'd get pretty tired walking. If my dad was there he'd pick me up and set me on his shoulders and by the time we arrived I would be sound asleep. The lane to the house was about fifty steps long. On the left there were great plum trees and about four walnut trees. These walnuts were large and had very thin shells and dried out quickly. Even I could break them in my little hands by squeezing two of them together. On the right-hand side of the yard there was a corn crib and a shed with a wagon and a horse-drawn sled.

Upon arriving at the house we would knock on the door and my aunt Julia or my uncle Janos would wake up and greet us. They would put two chairs together for me to lie on. The other folks would be sleeping in the back part of the house. My parents and my uncle and aunt would talk all night. My uncle would bring in a pitcher of wine and he and my dad would drink it by morning.

Uncle Janos worked in a tanning factory and I'll never forget the odour on his clothes when he came home from work. It was a pleasant scent for me as I liked the smell of new leather. He once taught me how to make shoelaces from a round disk of leather. I think I could still do that today.

~

I couldn't wait to see my cousins. I respected and idolized all of them. They had a blind old dog, Bundy. He had no problems getting around and came quickly when called. He was an amazing dog.

While I had seen cows before, I never saw one up close. The one my grandparents had was affectionately called Bettie and it was interesting to watch Juliska milk her. She managed to put all the milk in a pail with the exception of a few squirts for a cat. She boiled some to use and put the rest into a clay jug

37

(*Kocsog)* and let it turn into cottage cheese and butter. It was a process that fascinated me.

And now I have to repeat what I said before:

"That vineyard up on the hill had to be the most peaceful place on earth. I cherished the nights when Johnny and I laid on our backs in a haystack looking at the million stars above. He would tell me stories about the universe and the constellations - the Big Dipper and the Little Dipper, while the crickets chirped and a wolf howled behind the vineyard in the forest. I am misty-eyed as I write this.

Johnny taught me how to harness horses and hook them up to a wagon. He taught me how to make a windmill with June-bugs and how to chop down a tree with an axe. He taught me how to cut clover with a sickle and many other things we don't even do any more today. He showed me how to make a whistle from a willow twig. It was a meticulous job and you had to do it just right. I think I could still make one today. He was my best buddy in those days. I would listen to his fascinating stories until I fell asleep".

~

My grandparents' house was made of rammed earth approximately a hundred years ago. Johnny told me that this type of building was very common before the 1900's and was relatively easy to erect. He described the whole procedure to me which I have forgotten over the years. To be correct, I checked the exact steps on Wikipedia:

"*The house construction is started by levelling the ground and staking out the size of building. Forms were then made out of heavy planks and extended upward. They filled the forms with soil, packing it down with rams to create a wall a half metre wide and two-and-a-half metres high. Door and window frames were prepared ahead of construction and put into place as the work progressed. Water was added to dampen the soil, and chaff was mixed in to give more strength to the structure."*

As for the soil used, it may well have come from the wine cellar that would have been dug in the side of the hill at the same time the house was built. There was a barn attached to the house and it was made of the same materials and in the same way. The ceiling was hewn lumber, tightly fitted together. The roof was rye sheaves or cane.

I often wonder what a house would be like today if built in that old-fashioned way. Grandfather's house was warm in the winter and cool in the summer, without the need for any electronic devices. The floor was earthen. On some days, to make it look shiny and new, my grandmother would wash it with clay, similar to mopping a floor with water today.

The walls inside and outside were covered in white lime. My grandmother had wooden flower pots filled with geraniums sitting in the windows. I didn't particularly like the geraniums because to me they had an unpleasant fragrance.

There was an earthen oven in the kitchen where my grandmother used to bake bread. She made the loaves about half a metre round and she usually made four at a time using the yeast or culture left from the previous batch. She used dried corn stocks as fuel for the oven. The oven also served as a heat source in the winter.

The more well-to-do people had expensive ceramic stoves that were about a meter square and two and a half meters high. These were used exclusively for heating. When they were in use they were pretty hot to touch. Just one log in those stoves would keep the whole house warm all night and in the morning there would be just a cup of ashes left and the cinders inside the ashes would be just enough to restart the fire.

~

Grandfather's attic must have been well ventilated because that's where he kept his smoked pork shoulders, sausages (*kolbasz)* and bacon. All these meats were hung from hooks until they were used up. Sometimes Johnny and I went up there to break off pieces of sausage for a lunch.

In front of the house there was a pear tree that had the most delicious pears I ever ate. I could hardly wait for them to ripen every year. Even after the war was over, when my parents went to the farm for a visit, I would always ask; "Are the pears ripe yet?"

~

My grandmother grew cabbages for making her own sauerkraut. Her cabbages were different from the ones we are familiar with today. They were as big as watermelons and the leaves were thin and tightly packed. After she shredded them she added some peppercorns and bay leaves and salt on top. Everything stayed at room temperature. If I remember correctly, sometimes she even put a whole cabbage and hot red peppers into the barrel, mixing them with the shredded cabbage. She pressed it all down with thick boards and placed a heavy stone on top. The boards and the stone looked worn. I wonder how many generations have used those very same items.

When the curing process was done (in about three weeks) grandmother made cabbage rolls - they were awesome. I loved to pinch some sauerkraut to eat raw, a delicacy I enjoy even today, especially when I go to Hungary.

Once, here in Canada, I tried to make sauerkraut but messed it up big time. For starters I didn't have the right type of cabbage and my procedure was all wrong. When I lifted the lid on the small amount I had made I was surprised to see a culture of fuzzy white mold growing. It even smelled bad. You should probably make it in larger quantities for better results. Now I just stick to the so-so store-bought sauerkraut and I use fresh cabbage when I make my cabbage rolls. But they are still the best around in my opinion. Challenge me on that!

Chapter Five

Teacher recognises my name.

After mom and I left Budapest we went to the Onodi's where we stayed for awhile. Because she wanted to be closer to town, due to her pregnancy, she moved in with my other aunt Julia, Yany's mother. This is where my brother Attila was born August 8th 1944. Since I had more fun with Johnny at the vineyards, I stayed with him most of the time. I even helped with the chores. I did hoeing, corn husking and helped with the grain harvesting. I helped around a big thrashing machine that was powered by an old tractor with a long belt. I remember there was chaff dust flying everywhere. They made sheaves from the rye stocks which were carted away for use on roofs. I liked the grape harvest the best because I could help grandfather turn the screw on the grape press. It was fun to watch the juices flowing though the press slats. I remember Johnny making a siphon from cane and letting me take a swig or two from the fermenting vat. It got me tipsy.

~

My Jambor grandparents lived about two kilometres from Johnny's place. Sometimes when I went there he used to come with me. Instead of going the long way on the road, we boldly climbed down the side of a deep canyon grasping onto tree roots and vines. After crossing a small stream we had to climb up the other side the same way. It used to be exciting because I pretended to be Tarzan. However, I didn't swing on any vines, because they didn't seem strong enough to hold me.

~

Around the time my brother was born, school had started so I joined my mom at my aunt Julia's.

Russian soldiers had put up tents in her yard and occupied part of her house; but they allowed us to have our privacy. These soldiers must have liked children because one of them gave me a really fine harmonica. I learned to play it and cherished it for many years.

When the soldiers left I got busy gathering empty artillery shells, casings, weapons and all sorts of blown-up equipment that I found in aunt Julia's backyard. I even found a wandering horse once. It wasn't in good shape so I gave it away to a neighbour. I remember the soldiers not staying very long because the war was moving out of our area again.

~

Aunt Julia had a little shed in the yard where she kept corn stalks and when I went in there for something one day and found a sleek axe leaning against the corn stocks. I assumed a soldier had forgotten it; his loss, my gain. This was significant to me because you couldn't buy a sharp axe like that anywhere. We took it with us when we moved back to Budapest and used it for decades. From the way it was crafted it had to be either German or American made.

There was a tree in front of aunt Julia's house that I used to love to climb. Beneath it was a tiny stream that I used to dam with sand and then would watch the water break through and flow away again.

In front of Yany's old house. It was still standing in 2003.

That stream started at my Jambor grandparent's, where they shored it up to create a little well. Big crusty green bugs swam in the water and spider-like long-legged water bugs scooted on the surface. They were fun to watch. I wanted to catch them but they were lightning fast. On the other side of this 'well' there was a dirt road. It was used mainly by the locals to herd their sheep and cows and drive their horse-drawn wagons on. My grandparents had ducks and geese that often ventured onto this road. At one point, when the Russians had just pushed the Germans out of the territory, I witnessed a bunch of those birds getting shot by the soldiers. They brought them to my grandmother to clean and cook. I remember her not being too pleased about that.

~

The beginning of my grade three year was interesting. Often on my way to school, other children from isolated communities would join me and we'd walk five or six in a group. In the classroom before the teacher arrived, we'd have to stand up and repeat the multiplication table from one to ten out loud. One of the older boys always made sure everyone participated in this chorus.

I remember going to school in the winter with worn shoes and rags wrapped around my feet to try and keep the snow and cold out. Sometimes my mother would bake a couple of potatoes and put them in my pockets for warmth. This heat might have lasted a half an hour or so and we still had another half an hour to go before getting to the school. The snow couldn't have been too deep because I navigated the banks without any problems. I get a kick out of people today who say, "Oh, when I was young I had to walk two miles to school in three feet of snow and against the wind and up-hill all the way."

That school was an old building in the centre of the town of Nemedi. There was only one teacher in the school who taught all grades. There were usually about forty-five pupils in the same room. He remembered teaching my father he told me once. He must have remembered the name because there had been four Jambor boys and one girl attending that school over a fifteen year time frame. He even showed me the abacus and slate board my father had used.

My dad must have been one of the teacher's more favorite students because I've seen him in a photograph dressed up in a funny costume for some play or parade. It personified who my father was, which was a lot of fun. Yes, he must have been popular because he was admired by me, for sure. He was smart and always seemed to be on the ball.

One afternoon as my mates and I were walking home from school a fighter plane dove down and shot at us scaring the hell out of everybody. As the bullets kicked up dust on the road we huddled by a fence, terrified. The plane came back around a second time! It made no sense - who on earth would want to kill school kids?

On another day as we were coming out of school there was a commotion in the town square. The gendarmerie *(csendorok)* had caught a man stealing chickens from someone's yard. He was sentenced by the mayor right then and there. He received twelve lashes to his feet. We all stood around feeling sorry for him. He was screaming from the pain. Justice was quick and effective in those days and the police got respect. There were only two police officers in the village at that time. Today there would be a hundred. This is how my grade three began and ended, all too soon.

Chapter Six

*The war caught up with us. We play with
explosives.   I have my first dreadful cigarette.
Johnny is not strong enough to shoot with a machine
gun. I give him a hand.*

Towards the end of 1944 and early 1945 as bombs started falling all around us one more time, school closed and we returned to grandfather Onodi's place. I remember taking shelter in his wine cellar. At times when the explosions and shelling sounded distant, we would go outside and try to communicate with the soldiers we encountered.

Uncle Janos and Grandfather by the wine
cellar where we took cover through the battles.

During the time we stayed in wine cellar the hill changed hands between the Germans and the Russians several times. Since we didn't speak either language, we usually looked at the uniforms to determine who they were.

Some nights we watched the *katyushas* (multiple rocket launchers) blazing and hitting targets several kilometres down in the valley. Luckily, during all this bombing there was only one direct hit in front of our wine cellar. That explosion destroyed the cane-roofed shed that was attached to the cellar. It housed my grandfather's grape press, wooden tubs and tools. Some soldiers dug us out. I don't remember whether they were Russian or German. The house though, never had a direct hit.

After things settled down we moved back into the house and I travelled back and forth between my grandparents, sometimes jumping from the frying pan into the fire. There was a fierce war being fought everywhere all around us.

~

One night at my other grandparents home, the Jambor's, we heard a loud but muffled thud. It sounded like an explosion. Even though this boom was the loudest we'd ever heard, no one got up to check what had happened. In the morning we saw a bomb crater and were amazed at the size of it. The hole was less than ten metres from the back of the house! It had a circumference of at least twice the size of the house. Had the bomb fallen any closer all of us would have been killed. To this day I haven't been able to figure out why the house was not damaged that night or why its cane roof hadn't caught on fire.

In 2003 when I visited the old place by car, the earthen house was completely gone and the property was overgrown with shrubs and trees. A sand and gravel company had purchased the property and they were in the process of mining aggregates from the site. But the hillside looked familiar and I recognized the area where my uncle Paul and I had filled up some trenches with dirt and buried mortar shells and other ammunition. Since my visit was on a weekend and no workers were around, I couldn't warn anyone about possible dangerous explosives.

However an elderly-looking woman who lived across the road did come over to see what we were doing. She promised to tell the owners about the possible dangers on the site. I thought I recognized her until I realized she wasn't nearly as old as I was, she just looked it!

~

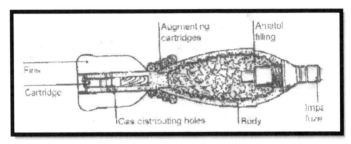

Picture of a modern mortar shell.
The older ones were not as sleek looking.

The bomb crater behind my grandfather's house was a good place to play. One day, a boy about my age blew off his left thumb while disassembling a mortar cartridge found there. We routinely took apart mortars so I can't imagine what went wrong. Usually we would remove the cartridge first and the nose fuses next. (Or the other way around).Then we would stand the shells up along the road, light the yellow dynamite and watch them burn intensely.

~

My cousin Johnny showed me how to spot and defuse land mines. Johnny might have been fifteen years old, give or take a year and I was eight. I've long forgotten what he actually taught me about those explosives. All I know is that he must have taught me well because I never got blown up.

In those days, Johnny became somewhat of an explosives expert. He would pick up land mines from the neighbouring farms and would take them to our canyon. After he thought he'd gathered up enough, he'd explode them with a device that he had built. We would be up on the bank of the canyon cheering after each explosion. One time I was lying on my stomach and the bank gave way under my chest. Fortunately I wasn't injured.

There was one land mine in particular and I believe it was German - that came in a neat, rectangular wooden box. I have always wondered how anyone could put such a nefarious device in such a handsome container. The trigger mechanism in the box accepted a Russian machine pistol casing. I would mount the pipe on a stock or grip and make a little pistol out of it. Then I'd pop the rounds without bullets. Ultimately I used up all the bullets, so I wrapped the pistol up and buried it in our yard and forgot about it. At a later time, I dug it back up to look at it and some of the parts had already rusted. I returned it to the hole in the ground, covered it with soil and left it there.

After the war moved from our territory I acquired all kinds of real pistols - German, Russian and Hungarian. One in particular I really liked. It was chrome-plated, probably a .22 calibre. I had that one for years, even after we moved back to Budapest.

Right about the time we were picking up land mines, I started smoking and I hate myself for that today. I think another boy had started and I just followed suit. I only smoked two or three homemade cigarettes once in a while. It wasn't a pleasant experience for me. I guess I was just curious. When I wanted to make a cigarette, it was pretty hard to find paper of any kind let alone cigarette paper.

Sometimes I rolled grandfather's virgin tobacco in a corn husk and tried to smoke it. That was even worse. I have to hand it to him - he was self-sufficient. He grew his own dreadful tobacco, dried it and cut it and kept it in a box on the master beam that supported the house. I remember having a hard time trying to reach that box from a chair. For daily use he kept his tobacco in a tanned bull's scrotum.

One time another cousin, Irma, my uncle Steve's daughter came to visit from Budapest. She was a smoker. She had a stuffing device for filling cigarette casings. She used grandfather's tobacco and put the finished cigarettes in the window to air. When she smoked them she coughed and told me that awful stuff would kill her. I lifted a few of her cigarettes for myself and smoked them. It was like smoking pure nicotine. It's a miracle I survived.

My grandfather smoked a long-stemmed pipe but only outside as he wasn't allowed to smoke in the house. In the house, he chewed that awful tarry substance that he would scrape out of his pipe with a jackknife. As a youngster I couldn't imagine how it must have tasted. When I became an adult I too smoked a pipe and became quite acquainted with that awful taste. In Canada, people chewed tobacco but it was an entirely different and pleasant substance.

~

I guess as kids we were not so much bold as we

were simply carefree. I get the jitters when I think of all the crazy things we did. By recounting the many dangerous situations I got myself into, I realize now that I could have been blown apart so many times.

We were always looking for creative ways to amuse ourselves and used the most wonderful array of deadly explosives and weapons we had at our disposal. We routinely knocked six to ten centimetre shells against trees to loosen up the live bullets. We had no idea whether they were armed or not. We would remove the spaghetti-like gunpowder called *cordite* and set the strands up in a line and light them. We used a lighter because matches were unavailable in those days. The strands burned fiercely with a hissing sound.

Sometimes we would weave the strands through tunnels, cross over water, go up and down little mounds and then branch them off into multiple avenues. Whoever could build the longest, most elaborate system was the winner in that game. The actual burn would last maybe a minute or two. We used different gun powders in our games. As I recall, the German rifle bullets were made of steel, all others were brass. The German gunpowder was square and the Russian was round. We had thousands of bullets of all descriptions at our disposal.

To the best of my knowledge, the Russian machine-pistol bullets came in a 15x15x15 centimetre tar paper wrapping. That was pretty heavy for a kid my age and we didn't like these particular bullets because they were too short to hang on to. We had to push down on them in order to get the bullets loosened from the casings. On the other hand, because the bullets were short they were easier to pound into logs.

We had a length of angle iron from an old bed that had holes in it - perfect for our purposes. After we emptied the casings we drove them into logs like nails.

Then with the inner corner of an axe, we would pop those casings. The person with the most pops in succession would win that game. Whoever had the best eye-hand coordination usually won. I have to say that I succeeded in winning most of the time.

We found yellow incendiary disks in the forest and we played with them as if they were toys. These disks had about a three centimetre hole in the centre and would catch fire in the sun. I had heard about kids finding dolls and other toys that exploded when handled and couldn't imagine which of the Allied Forces would drop those things. I thought they weren't supposed to hurt the children.

We had hand grenades of all descriptions some small and some large. Some had knobs. The German and Hungarian grenades had handles and other grenades had one or more red circles on them - Russian perhaps? We all had our own cache of weapons to showcase. We traded them like kids trade baseball cards today. Some hand grenades came in a flat wooden box with maybe a dozen to a box.

In the village, kids were sometimes blown apart by exploding hand grenades. But none of my friends or family members ever were. However, I did hear of a man's stomach being blown open while trying to get the flintstone out of a mortar. Flintstones for lighters were very hard to find in those days. My cousin Juliska knew him. He was a neighbour. He managed to carry his stomach home in his hands which was unbelievable. There was no doctor around and no one else could help him. He died a horrible death - all for the sake of trying to get a piece of flint for a lighter.

We would get an empty ten centimetre artillery shell and fill it up with a cocktail of gunpowder and live bullets. We would then throw a burning ember into it and watch the whole thing light on fire. It would burn as high as the sky and made a *whooshing* noise. The bullets would start to explode, yet none of them would break through the artillery shell. At first we used to watch cautiously from behind a half-metre thick wall but when we found them to be benign, we would watch them unshielded, from a short distance.

I shiver when I think about how crazy we were - most of us were only eight to ten years old. It was all great entertainment that we designed and staged ourselves. If one of those shells had ever tipped in our direction we would have been burned or would have burned a house down. Let's face it - we were lucky as hell to have survived these escapades. I was just a kid without fear.

Some might ask where our parents were. They must have been either at work in the village or out in the pastures guarding the farm animals. For the most part, children were left alone to pursue their games, dangerous as they were.

One time, Johnny got hold of a machine gun - did we ever have fun with that! When he realized he wasn't strong enough to control it, he set it up on its tripod and tied it to a tree. Then while still holding onto it, he pulled the trigger. It made one heck of a racket! I was feeding the belt from a metal box. When I looked up at him, it was funny to watch his teeth rattling to the rhythm of the gun. I even remember the tree we tied the gun to because I saw some plums on it. There were about ten of those plum trees lining a laneway up to the vineyard where beautiful white Riesling grapes were growing.

Not far from that lane Johnny once buried several bottles of white wine. I didn't know why since he could have had all the wine he wanted from grandfather's barrels. Later however, after we found out that all the neighbouring cellars (about fifty of them) had been broken into and the barrels had been machine-gunned, those bottles came in handy. I don't remember who did the shooting - Germans or Russians - but whoever did, certainly didn't want the other to have the wine.

Chapter Seven

*We return to Budapest. I am a multi-billionaire –
in obsolete currency. Uncle Steve lives on the same
street. I get the shock of my life and 'die' a second time.
I almost freeze to death.*

In the spring of 1945, we returned to Budapest to the
suburb of Lorinc (eighteenth district of Budapest).
We travelled in a horse-drawn wagon driven by
Johnny's father. The trip took three days.

Since it was spring time the snow was melting.
During our trip to Budapest we saw many shallow
graves with an arm or leg exposed. The stench was
sickening. Some nights we would camp in a barn on a
farm, sleeping on straw or hay. Attila my little brother
was around nine months and needed milk. The farmer
would bring him goat's milk.

I watched the same farmer collect urine from
uncle Onodi's pregnant mare. The urine was used in
homemade medicine that alleviated the symptoms of
menopause. Interestingly this medication was already in
use in 1945. Today they make *Premarin* from mare's
urine for the same purpose.

We crossed the Danube River from Buda to Pest
on pontoons because all the bridges had been destroyed.
I can still picture my uncle struggling to hang onto the
horse reins. There were several Russian soldiers around
and they gave him a hand. Still, my mom and I were
scared to death. Our fear was due to neither of us
knowing how to swim. If we were to fall into the river
we would have drowned for sure. It took about twenty
minutes to reach the other side of this makeshift bridge.
It was a long twenty minutes for all of us.

~

When we arrived at 18 Barcsay Street to a half demolished little house, my father was already there fixing it up. His older brother Steven, (*Pistabacsi)* lived at 11 Barcsay Street, but he wasn't able to help my father because he was gravely ill with tuberculosis. He had been a prisoner of war and due to his illness was allowed to come home ahead of the other prisoners. I remember on his last day we went over to his house to say goodbye and we all touched his arm and kissed him. My aunt stayed with him until he passed away. I think he was only forty years old. We were all deeply saddened.

~

While our house wasn't much to look at, it was ours. My father bought it from a relative who didn't have the expertise to fix it. It was one of the houses on the street that had been hit by a bomb and had to be rebuilt entirely.

There was an apple tree in the yard and I was climbing it one day checking to see if the apples were ripe - they weren't. However, there were some cherry trees at Joe Vinklar's. His father's place was just past an empty lot to the right of our house. Joe noticed me in the tree and called me over. Once we got acquainted he gave me some of his cherries. They were yellow in colour, the early type.

We immediately became friends, a friendship that lasted a lifetime. Joe was two years older. He was eleven and I was nine. He was born February 8, 1934. He is on my mind a lot these days because when I called him on his birthday not long ago, his wife Eta told me that he'd had a stroke.

Joe had taught me what I believed was everything I needed to know at that young age. But I taught him a few things too, namely a little something about explosives. One day Joe had a fire going in his

57

yard and I noticed the smoke and hollered over asking what he was up to. He said he was burning some branches and wood and I asked if I could come over. He said sure.

I filled a small bottle with alcohol from my father's jar which he kept for cleaning purposes. Joe was just as mischievous as I was and when I told him what I had in mind he went along with my plan without any argument. I of course, wanted to find out if the alcohol would explode in the fire. I threw the bottle in and we waited. We stepped back a few paces - just in time, too. That little bottle exploded with a deafening noise. We were astonished and thought all the windows had shattered. We also thought the neighbours would come running to see what had happened. However, the windows didn't break and nobody came running. Our ears were ringing for a few hours though and we got an education - even little bottles of alcohol can make a big noise when thrown into a fire.

~

Joe lived in a large house with his father, his grandparents as well as an uncle and his family. Joe's parents were divorced. We had a lot of fun playing hide and seek on that property when nobody was home. The house had a large attic with sand on the floor for insulation. It was accessible from the outside and we used to hide there. The huge backyard was full of tall weeds which were great for hiding in. For me, it was just like being in a jungle. At night when I went to sleep I always visualized Joe's backyard full of monkeys, leopards and tigers and Tarzan swinging on vines. African wildlife fascinated me - maybe I should have become an explorer! I used to draw gorillas and snakes in school all the time. My brother saved some of my drawings.

There was a Bulgarian garden behind our houses

and all the kids picked some tomatoes from there when they ripened. We ate them with salt and boy, were they ever good!

~

That same summer I had the opportunity to work for our neighbour Mr. Pup (*Pup bacsi*). He had a belt buckle shop across the street from us. He gave me the tedious job of cutting wires to length and bending them into squares in a hand-operated device. I think I was  making the equivalent of five cents an hour in Canadian money. As I remember, it was an incredibly boring job. Each time I bent a wire into a U, I had to take the bending arms out and turn them upside down to finish bending the U into a square. It occurred to me after doing that about a thousand times, that if I took a straight wire and placed it into the second position, I could form the whole square with one motion. I surprised myself and bewildered Mr. Pup. He had likely bent a million of them himself the old way. He gave me a penny raise, even though this innovation cut the manufacturing time to one-quarter. However, those earnings became worthless.

This all happened during the time when Hungary's currency collapsed. Hungary had the world's greatest inflation. This is recorded in the book of world records. Just imagine that a box of matches cost a trillion Pengos. Hungarian money couldn't be translated into dollars and cents because actually it had no value at all.

~

When I was not working, I was playing soccer. One day while playing on our soccer field we heard loud noises that reminded us of tanks. And that's what they were; T-34 Russian tanks. They were coming down the street and the soldiers sitting on top of the tanks were throwing handfuls of bills into the air. We all rushed into the street to grab as many as we could. We quickly realized that the bills were worthless. But at least we had something to start fires with in our stoves.

~

While we were bending belt buckles more efficiently in Mr. Pup's shop, other jobs also needed upgrading. For instance, Mr. Pup had a hexagonal wooden drum for shining the metal parts he made. He did this by first putting sawdust into the drum, then adding stones and finally adding the buckles. He would close the drum lid and start turning it around and around about a thousand times. I wasn't strong enough to do the cranking so Mr. Pup was stuck with that job. It should have been done using an electric motor, but I guess he didn't have the money for that kind of upgrade. The rotating sawdust and stones made his parts shiny and he would take them to his customers the same day. I can still envision him today, pushing his bicycle with a couple of heavy bags draped over the crossbar.

I wasn't knowledgeable enough yet to redesign his shop, but one thing was for sure, my life as an innovator and mechanical designer was determined then and there.

~

One day Mr. Pup told me to change a burned-out light bulb. In Europe, the current is DC and is two hundred and twenty volts. The bulb was over a metal clad work bench. To reach it I had to climb onto that bench. At the age of nine I was just a little guy - maybe a hundred and thirty centimetres and weighing about thirty-five kilograms - but full of pep and vigour. In order to reach the bulb I had to hang onto its cord with my left hand and turn the bulb with my right. That bulb had to have been there since the 'beginning of time' because it felt like it was welded into the socket and didn't want to come loose. When I reached a little higher with my right hand I must have touched the bare socket because I got the shock of my life. I was knocked unconscious and fell to the floor.

I don't know what all happened but what I can say is that I was in the shop the next day and I am here today. This *minor* incident could have been much worse and it taught me an important lesson - always treat electricity with respect.

~

Mr. Pup had some relatives in the western part of Hungary in Ikervar. Whenever his little nephew Mike *(Mishi)*, would come to visit, we would play together and we became good friends. During the school break in the summer of 1946 I was ten years old and was thinking of getting a better job. Something I could sink my teeth into. My parents suggested that I go and help a relative who was building his house. The wages were good but the job didn't last long. I was laid off. The currency had become stabilized and money was now named *Forints*. I still had some time left in my summer recess so, I decided to visit Mike in Ikervar.

I was supposed to board the train the next day. Unfortunately while bicycling home from a swimming trip to the Danube River, I got a flat tire and fell off my bike injuring my left hand. I have to mention that the river was so badly polluted that we had oil all over our bodies and we never went there to swim again. I didn't tell my mother because had she found out, she would never have let me leave to go and see my friend Mike. I suffered with excruciating pain through the night and didn't get any sleep. I got up in the morning, said goodbye and left for the train station.

When I arrived at my destination I was in agonizing pain. Mike's mother noticed my swollen hand and after I told her what had happened she wrapped my hand in a vinegar-soaked towel and sent me to bed. When I woke up the next day, to my greatest surprise there was no sign of any swelling. And there was no more pain either.

~

Mike's dad was a blacksmith and had his own shop. He was a large, hairy man with gentle facial features. I'll never forget the good times I had there. He taught me how to make horseshoes, how to strike iron while it was hot - in tandem no less - and how to make rims for wooden buggy wheels.

We went bowling in a dirt alley and went *bathing* in a rice paddy where the water was over forty degrees Celsius. All kinds of people were frolicking there. Men and women wore just a little towel on a string at the front and nothing in the back. Weird or what?

~

Now I'll describe my second *major* death-defeating incident.

Three or four days into my vacation at Mike's, a bunch of kids went down to a local creek named Raba which is a revered national stream. The stream water wasn't as warm as the rice paddy and it was cloudy. Everybody was splashing around, having fun. I didn't know how to swim yet and thought I didn't need to know because there was a large log submerged in the water that I could hang onto. The kids were diving into the water from a bridge which was only a couple of meters high. The water had pooled under this bridge. It looked like it would be fun to dive from there. They told me not to worry, just dive in. They would help me if I needed to be rescued. They rescued me alright. When I dove in I smashed my head right on that submerged log. The next thing I remember I was being held up in the air by two kids. They were holding me upside down and I was puking water. That night I slept with a vinegar-soaked towel on my head.

My trip home was uneventful. The train stopped at every village. The one hundred and fifty kilometres from Ikervar to Budapest took about eight hours. I spent another two hours on a streetcar from the train station to my house. I arrived home around midnight.

~

Life was simple in small towns like Ikervar. It was certainly better than in the city, especially as far as food was concerned. In Budapest most everything was rationed and usually out of stock. Many stores had nothing in them, only bare shelves. I spent numerous hours standing in line in the early hours of the morning - sometimes as early as two a.m. - just for meagre portions of bread, sugar, or meat. My shoes were worn-out and I had no winter clothes. Sometimes I almost froze to death while waiting in line. It was next to impossible to find fruits or vegetables. It was terribly upsetting when the store ran out of a product just before I got to the door and unfortunately this happened a lot.

Many times a store would sell potatoes and most of them would be frozen. Times were so difficult that even the store owners couldn't afford to heat their premises. When I arrived home with a bag of frozen potatoes my mom would just swallow hard and roll her eyes. I didn't know any better. How is a child supposed to check if a potato is frozen? My poor mom had no food to cook for my father who had to go to work. His usual fare was a couple slices of bread and a piece of bacon or some balogna. Maybe twice a month we were able to get a hundred milligrams of butter. When there was no butter, my mom would spread lard or jam on bread.

We purchased all our food with food stamps. Bread used to be the hardest to get! Usually the line-ups at the bakery were half a kilometre long. It didn't matter how much bread they made, they always sold out. The type and amount of bread available depended upon the flour on hand. The bakers would make the bread from whichever flour they could get a hold of whether it was rye, corn or oats. Numerous times there would be rodent excrement, stones or wood chips in the bread.

Dry beans and peas were the worst for clumps of mud and stones and my mother always cautioned me to check the beans and peas closely - a practice I follow even today. You would be surprised how many stones I picked out from loose, processed dry beans when I was a boy. I shiver when I think of biting onto a stone and breaking a tooth while eating bean soup. Nowadays most people don't buy dried beans anymore because canned or packaged soups are more convenient.

Good milk was a scarce item as well, especially in the winter. And it was usually frozen. Sometimes the frozen milk would give us an upset stomach. Some elderly folks sold their milk stamps for money so they could buy a bar of soap instead - if they could find any.

Soap was almost impossible to find.

I swear our clothes were made of paper, or worse, because they wore out so fast. Even in 1951 six years after the war had ended, I remember going to the store with my mother to buy my graduation suit for grade eight and getting it two sizes larger than I needed in order to allow for shrinkage.

~

Starting back in grade four or five, an organization, either the Red Cross or UNICEF, began bringing chocolate milk to our schools in the mornings and each child was given half a litre. At noon we were given soup and cheese. This lasted through grade eight. Without this program many of us would have starved to death.

Chapter Eight

Early Woodstock at (Margaret Island). Uncle Steve passes away. Steven Jr. becomes head of the household. He always acted like he was my older brother.

After uncle Steven died, Steven Jr. became the head of that Jambor family. Steven Jr. and I became good buddies and he took me to a lot of places - concerts, movies, theatres and museums that I wouldn't have been able to attend had I been alone. One day we went to see a popular band we both liked. This became a special day. They played on *Margit Sziget* (Margaret Island) in an outside amphitheatre. The admission was reasonable and the entertainment was out of this world. Since the bands came from abroad we couldn't understand the lyrics but we adored the music they played. I think many of the bands were Italian and French, possibly English as well. To me they were the epitome of early rock-and-roll!

I also remember the time Steve took me to an American movie. Amazingly enough we could view foreign movies for several years after the Russians took over. Movies were cheap at two cents a show - about the only thing that was cheap. They were good movies from all over the world. I remember *The Hunchback of Notre Dame, Wages of Fear,* and *We Were Soldiers* to name a few. The American movie Steve took me to was rated "adult with parental guidance." I didn't understand why parental guidance was such a big deal.

~

Steve was working in a nearby factory, a huge machine shop that I believe was called Red Star and he asked me to join their vibrant youth club. The company sponsored numerous activities such as gymnastics, soccer, basketball, wrestling and boxing. These youth clubs were quite common. Almost all major employers sponsored them, most likely to give their employees and families something to do and to help keep them in shape.

In the youth club we could even learn target-shooting and hand-grenade throwing. They had regular trainers on staff. I hadn't realized there was a special technique to throwing a hand grenade - I had always just pulled the pin, counted to three, and heaved it. That was one *art* I already knew. I decided to try boxing which turned out to be the worst decision I could have made.

In order to make it onto a team I had to pass a test. The trainers put me up against older kids who beat the daylights out of me. Steve once told me the trainers always put novices up against the more experienced boxers to find out if they were tough enough to be considered for the team. I wasn't. I would get beat up so badly and often ended up with either two black eyes or a bloody nose. I believe this was the time I had some unbelievable headaches. Even though I was thirteen or fourteen years old I went home crying almost every time. My boxing days were short-lived. I changed to soccer which I was already familiar with, having played in our little park at the end of my street.

~

Steve got married a couple of years later and I was his best man. The wedding was large and was held at his house. It lasted Saturday, Sunday and Monday and I was present the entire time. In fact, I remember getting him black coffee to ease his hangover pain. I don't remember if we even slept! Steve's wedding was indeed a memorable occasion on our street.

Unfortunately the passing of the years were not

kind to Steve. Like all young men, he had to serve in the Hungarian army for two years and was drafted around 1950. Everyone during these times had to work very hard for minimal wages and had to pay for all the *communist five-year plans.* There were three-year plans and five-year plans and you could subscribe to any or all of them and they were essentially deducted from your wages. You loaned a hundred, two hundred, or five hundred *Forints* to the National Bank without interest and got your loaned amount back after your plan expired. But by that time the money had devalued by fifty per cent or more. However, if you didn't subscribe you were classified an enemy of the nation as well as an enemy of the *heroic* communist party, and that was bad. Worker wages were barely enough to exist on, similar to working for minimum wage would be today.

There was a lot of misery in those days trying to make a living under such a dominant regime.

Chapter Nine

Don't try this at home, in school or anywhere.
I go to school and play on real T-34 Russian tanks. I
have a minor incident twice. A Russian soldier really
scares me.
I wipe the floor with two bullies.

Whenever my father had free time he worked on our little house that had been damaged by an explosion during the war at 18 Barcsay Street. It was located between two vacant lots. The one on the left had terrible goat head thorns (*kiralydinnye)* growing all over it; the one on the right had fruit trees. Beyond the fruit-treed lot was my best friend Joe's house.

The vacant lot with the goat head thorns at number 16 also had some large ground-dwelling spiders which were probably poisonous to humans. They never affected our cat though. It hunted and ate them. I watched that cat sit patiently for hours on end by a hole waiting for a spider to come out. And when it did, that spider was snatched up in a second! Unfortunately my father had to kill that spider-eating cat one day because it was foaming at the mouth and attacking my brother Attila. I can only guess that it had rabies.

The owner of the lot with the goat-head thorns was someone I never met, even though he had a nice wooden shed on the lot, which I assumed could have been rented out for storage

There was a picket fence on either side of the property where we lived. However, the property down the street from us at number 14 had a heavy chain-link fence in front of it complete with an iron gate. Two families resided there. There was an older couple, the Kovacs, and a younger family, the Olahs, who were about the same age as my parents.

The Kovacs lived in the front building, an unfinished structure that was made entirely of concrete. I think only two of the four rooms were livable. There was a tiny house behind this unfinished building which was parallel to our house. This property backed onto the Bulgarian vegetable garden I have mentioned before.

The Olah family had four children—two boys and two girls. I cannot imagine how they all fit into their small house. The kitchen was only about three metres by three metres and there was only one bedroom which was approximately three metres by four metres. All the Olah kids were younger than myself but I became good friends with George (*Gyuszi)* who was only a year younger. His brother's name was Frank and the two sisters were Barbara (*Baba*) and Giselle (*Gizi)*. Mr. and Mrs. Olah never allowed their children beyond the fenced yard other than to attend school. George and I began communicating over the empty lot. One day we came up with the idea of digging a tunnel between his house and mine - a distance of about fifteen metres - so he could sneak out unseen by the Kovacs when his parents weren't home and to avoid the deadly spiders and pervasive goat head thorns that permeated the lot between us. These thorns were capable of puncturing bicycle tires.

We dug the tunnel when our parents weren't home and covered the entries with boards, using some of the dug-out sand to camouflage the boards. The rest we spread around the yard. This was a large project for two young boys - it took weeks – and were we ever lucky! During the digging of the small hole which was about the size of the opening of a bushel basket, we never had a cave-in. The weeds in the soil above must have held the dirt together. The tunnel was only big enough for one person to crawl through at a time. When George crawled to my place we smoked cigarettes and talked about our experiences in school. But we could only use our tunnel when there was no one home which only happened a few times a month.

I was playing outside one day when Mrs. Olah came over to chat with my mother. She sat outside in front of our kitchen right above the entrance to my tunnel. I was having a fit! Suddenly, the inevitable happened. Mrs. Olah's chair sunk into the opening of the tunnel and tipped over. She didn't hurt herself but the hole was discovered. When my mother questioned me, I told her I had dug the hole to get some nice yellow sand. Surprisingly, I got away with that story. My mother filled the opening with trash and ashes from the stove. When I informed George about the near disaster, he hurriedly filled his entrance up too.

~

One time when both our parents were away, George and I were playing hide-and-seek with a bunch of kids from the neighbourhood. We played at my house even though there weren't many good hiding places. There was however, the wood shed, the outhouse, some grape bushes and under the bed inside the house. This particular time I decided to venture onto the roof and hide behind the chimney. When discovered, I tried to jump off the roof onto a nearby tree - like Tarzan - but I missed the branch and fell, dislocating my right thumb. I remember the pain was unbearable and worse than that, I couldn't say anything about it since we were not allowed on the roof because it had clay tile shingles that broke easily. Even though I lived through that adventure I still have a bump on my thumb, a reminder of that mishap.

~

In order to make more wages and receive promotions at work, you had to be a member of the communist party. George's father was a decorated *Communist Hero.* Factories used to reward these outstanding workers with medals or badges, certificates, money or special privileges. Mr. Olah, being an exemplary worker, was a *Revolutionary Guard,* a title that meant nothing other than the fact that he would receive bonuses for reporting un-party-like behaviour. Because of this status he was given the opportunity to create something unique, after regular working hours of course. He decided to make an air rifle.

When he finished the air rifle he brought the gun home and George got hold of it. He asked me to come to his gate because he wanted to show it to me. I admired it through the chain link fence but he wouldn't let me touch it. The gun had no stock and George had a hard time priming it. When I asked him if he could shoot with it, he told me he had no ammunition.

I noticed ripening berries on some bushes on his side of the fence and I began to think that the seeds in those berries would probably fit into the gun's chamber. They did. George started shooting at objects and whether by accident or by design, he aimed at my bare chest and squeezed the trigger. I was astounded when the berry hit me as it knocked me to the ground. That was the only time in my life anyone shot me. The seed went right under my skin. George was just as shocked as I was, maybe even more so. I believe he thought I was dead. Fortunately, I wasn't. Despite this *minor* incident we remained friends but I never confronted him when he had a gun in his hand.

~

When I went to school that fall several things happened in rapid succession. My school was on *Aponyi Albert Utca* which later became *Hengersor Utca*. To the right of this elementary school was a college and next to that was a large refurbishing factory. The office of that factory faced the soccer field where Puskas and Kocsis, the legendary soccer players, practised. These were the athletes that helped defeat the English team in the 1955 World Cup finals.

In the factory office there was someone who sang and played the same tune on the piano all the time. The song was about an old woman who had to hear 'this song' in order to fall asleep. It was so strange. It was a simple little song with a catchy tune. I remember it even today and I imagine I am not the only one. I doubt I will ever forget it.

Behind the schools and the factory there was a huge vacant lot with hundreds of T-34 Russian tanks. They were all damaged, either on the inside or on the outside. There was no fence around these tanks - making the lot a heaven for school kids. We climbed in and out of them, day after day, at lunch time and after school. We scavenged prisms, gauges, bullets and any interesting gadgets that we could play with.

Leading up to this area was a rail line that supplied repair parts for the tanks and transported these tanks out when they were refurbished. At our noon recess, for the sake of sheer amusement, we would push empty wagons up a slight incline on that rail line track and then would roll them back down until they bumped into other wagons stationed near the street. To make this game even more interesting we loaded the tracks with gunpowder and bullets of all sorts - facing them away from us of course. How we screamed with joy when they exploded!

One time there was only a few of us pushing a wagon up the hill and it started to roll backwards. My head happened to be right in line with the bumpers. Had it not been for one alert schoolmate, I would have wound up with a pancake-thin head! I was already beginning to feel the bumpers on my ears when he pulled me away from that near disaster. I shiver whenever I think of this *minor* incident.

Shortly after that, the Russians put up a fence and a gate across the tracks and kept the wagons on the incline away from the school. We were not allowed to walk through the field of tanks anymore and we couldn't play with the railroad cars either. They posted sentries that walked the property and they caught me once with some useless tank part. I was scared to death when they made me kneel in front of the captain's office. I was upset that I had been caught. They pointed a machine pistol at my back and although I knew they wouldn't shoot me (they were just trying to scare me) I promised I would never enter the property again. I never did.

~

School was a real pleasure for me and I learned a lot. In grades three and four we were taught German. After that we had to take Russian. I remember very little of either language today.

One of the boys in my class was a bit weird. He would always do something to draw attention to himself, especially from the girls. One time he sat in the window with a magnifying glass and burned spots on his arm until they puffed up into blisters. It was an unpleasant odour and I still remember that smell in my nose to this day.

During recess one day, he started hitting his arm with a ruler and got his skin to puff up in welts each place he hit. Another time he wanted to scare us by throwing some bullet casings in the stove. He expected them to explode right away but they didn't. When the teacher came in and began the lesson, the casings suddenly, like a machine gun, started going off. It scared the hell out of the teacher and everyone else and I think my classmate was suspended. I can't quite recall. I guess I would say it was a good prank back then, but imagine what would happen to a student if they did that today.

~

I had an encounter with two bullies when I was in grade seven, both of whom I fought and beat up on different occasions. I remember the whole class cheering for me and egging me on and those were the only times in my life when I felt like a real hero. One of those bullies probably remembers me forever because I broke his front tooth. He and his mother had the audacity to come to our house to complain to my mother about me beating him up. He was almost twice my size! I was a skinny kid, but I took no bull from anyone - an attitude I have maintained throughout my life.

Chapter Ten

Our favourite relative comes home from Siberia.
A rooster is also a good play pal. Yany gets promoted
then lands in jail. My father is unfairly incarcerated.

O ne day in 1949, Yany, our favourite relative came home from Siberia. I was playing in the street when I saw him walking down the middle of the road looking for our house number. He had been

in a POW camp in Siberia and was reduced to skin and bone. The work was hard in this proverbial Russian "salt mine" - they had no days off. It was always cold and the prisoners had inadequate clothing, shoes and food. Many died just trying to survive. Yany stayed with us for quite a while and I remember he had to watch his calorie intake, which wasn't too tough since we didn't have much food around in those days anyway. He brought my mother a Catholic motif of Jesus on the cross that he had built inside a small bottle. I still have it.

Yany was a butcher by trade and I believe he was the best butcher I've ever known.

Later, after he got on his feet he moved to Szakesfehervar, about sixty kilometres away and we were always overjoyed when he came for a visit. He would bring us some sausages or salami, which in my opinion were the best. On these occasions Yany and my father would talk day and night. Yany talked about his unbearable suffering in the Russian Gulag and my dad talked about his misadventures during the war. There was enough to talk about forever, for the both of them.

Amongst all the stories they exchanged there was one that stood out in my memory. It was a story about my father and the train he worked on. This event took place during the war in either 1942 or 1943. His locomotive was strafed by warplanes, something that happened quite frequently. While it was still moving, he jumped off hoping to hide amongst the reeds in a nearby trench. However, when he rolled into what he thought was a shallow ditch, he got the surprise of his life; he sank straight down. The ditch was full of raw sewage that had crusted over! Luckily, it only reached his chin. After the raid was over his colleagues found him and rescued him with a rope. Otherwise, he might have drowned and never been found. The locomotive was riddled with bullets, but before the boiler lost all its water he was able to use some of it to wash the sewage off his body. Still, he said he smelled like a sewer rat. In his memory, I have written a novel about a train. It is called *The Passengers.*

My father standing on the train he worked on.
(Note the bumper!)

~

Yany and my father were a real pair when they got together. When they would drink, or as I like to say, *dip into the sauce,* and they would start singing old Hungarian songs. In the process they would get emotional and incredibly mischievous, sometimes even with me. There is one particular day I'll never forget.

Yany and my father 'dipping into the sauce'

I was thirteen or fourteen when I had a pet rooster and we played together all the time. He followed me everywhere I went, constantly clucking. I think he must have been lonely because we only had him, no hens. I dug some holes for him and he scratched in them until he found a worm. He always followed me until I fed him something and when I ran away from him he flew after me. When you are a child, you can play with anything.

Yany and my father got me and the rooster drunk on moonshine (*palinka*). The rooster started crowing and began tripping over its wings. The two pranksters laughed hysterically. I don't remember how I managed, but I got into the bedroom and opened the window and barfed all over Yany. Unfortunately he was wearing a brand new suit. My mother gave me heck but she gave the two of them hell for getting me drunk in the first place. The next thing I remember, I was eating chicken - my rooster! My heart is still broken over that rooster.

~

When I was little, Yany loved to hear me singing an old Hungarian song about a forest, even though I couldn't properly pronounce one of the words. Maybe that's the part he liked. I learned countless songs over the years and showed off with them every time the family got together. It's amazing how most nationalities can have a good time singing old songs without instrumental backup, just voices. The lack of instruments never bothered me, I always thought that someday I'd play one, but I never did - not a real one anyway.

From an early age I was experimenting with different instruments, sometimes as complicated as wax paper and a comb. I know that doesn't sound too extraordinary, but put yourself in my position. After the war, I didn't even have a fine-tooth comb or wax paper. Of course I could have used spoons or pots and pans, but in my opinion they didn't suit old Hungarian songs.

~

By the time I was fourteen I had become a pretty heavy smoker. I sustained my awful habit with money I made working at various jobs during the summer, one of which was at a brick factory. My job was to clear weeds from plots to make room for *green* bricks fresh out of the slicer, which had to be stacked out in the sun to dry. This job was about as tough as I've ever had in my entire life. Imagine hoeing pervasive weeds from hard clay ground all day. That was a pretty physical job, even for me, and I considered myself pretty tough.

There was only one job harder than the weeding - emptying the kilns. The freshly fired ceramic bricks were removed five bricks at a time by a dozen guys working in a line. The first person grabbed the bricks and handed them to the second and so on down the line and the last person stacked them. Because the temperature was around fifty degrees Celsius, no one could stand to be inside for more than a short time. Usually the first person changed places with the last person every three minutes. Perspiration ran down everyone like water from a tap. And since we didn't have gloves our fingertips wore off in the first fifteen minutes. I could have robbed banks - the police would never have been able to trace me through my fingerprints.

Because I soldiered on doing all the toughest jobs they gave me without complaining, the boss asked me one day if I could paint signs. Could I paint signs! My father was a decorator in a porcelain factory I informed him. Not that his job had anything to do with this one, but maybe I got that promotion to paint communist slogans on banners, walls and solid brick fences because of it. I had that sign painting job for years at that factory and almost made more money than my father.

~

After the time my rooster became dinner, Yany was promoted to being a buyer for a national meat processor and was doing a little business - buying animals for private farms and butchers - on the side. He got fingered and landed in jail. Running his own business wasn't the problem - it was the fact that he didn't belong to the communist party.

When I was around fifteen, my father was a fireman on a locomotive. He and the engineer both got jailed for letting people take coal from train wagons - allegedly. In those days no one had any fuel to heat or cook with. Neither my father nor the engineer had noticed anyone taking coal and neither one of them was in charge of security.

I remember seeing two civilian AVO (Communist State Police), coming to our house. One of them slapped my father in the face. He lived, but only because they had guns. My father was a tough guy and could easily have beaten the daylights out of both of them. Those cops also took my inflated tractor tire tube that I kept for swimming. I think they thought my father had stolen it from somewhere. They returned the tube in a few weeks still inflated, but they took my father to jail in handcuffs. My mother and I broke down in tears.

There was never a trial of any kind - sadly, people would just *disappear*. I felt it was unjust, but typical of the communists that someone would come to our house, pick my father up and take him away. This was the kind of thing that happened day after day everywhere during these times. My mother was terribly distraught because she had no idea how we were going to survive. She would have to make a decision on whether to find a job or not - and jobs were few and far between.

Life had been hard enough living on my father's small salary and it became unbearable without his income. Nobody had any money to spend. Mr. Pup only needed me occasionally and my mother would do household duties for people that had to work all day - she would clean for some, iron for others, and babysit for young mothers. Somehow she managed to scrape together enough money to pay the mortgage. I had to cut my movies even though they only cost two cents. The little money I made at odd jobs and my mother's meagre house cleaning pennies kept us at the very bottom of existence. I remember my mom travelling the one hundred and twenty kilometres to my grandparents by train, three or four times a month to barter items the country folk couldn't get. Things like clothing, shoes and dresses in exchange for food like bacon, eggs, etc. She would return home and sell them to the neighbours. Even still, we barely had enough to survive.

Once in a while, we scraped together enough money for streetcar tickets and went to see my dad. He was on forced labour at the bombed out Parliament building. Forced labour meant he had to do any job they asked of him, including disposing of executed prisoners. He never talked much about that. The Parliament building, like most buildings in Budapest, had been badly damaged during the war and many other structures had been destroyed. The labourers were often tasked with removing debris. Once they even found people still in a basement bunker - seven or eight years after the war. They had all kinds of canned food and even water that ran from taps. My father's sentence lasted nine months and a few years later both he and the engineer were exonerated.

Charles Eric Jambor

Chapter Eleven

*I race bikes, play soccer while my friend
agonizes on the violin. We all suffer listening to his
horrendous music. My brother picks wild mushrooms. A
gang comes to kill me.
I 'die' the third time.*

Life on Barcsay Street was fairly simple, but I
made it a little more interesting by inventing
games that a lot of us could play. For instance; I
mapped out bicycle racing tracks throughout several
streets – not as complicated as we see on TV nowadays,
but none the less as challenging. Our bikes were heavy
and clumsy and had bad tires. They were hard to paddle.
Some tires had two or three clumpy patches. To keep
time we used alarm clocks. The older boys usually won
in these races.

~

After my father was released from jail he went
back to work. We were so poor that we didn't have the
money to run electricity into the house. We needed
another pole for the electricity but couldn't afford it. We
also had no running water but neither did anyone else on
our street. I had to go for water most of the time which
was only available about a kilometre from our house.

In the summertime I had to go past the park
where my friends would be playing soccer. Sometimes
on my way back they would overwhelm me and drink
most of my water, laughing no less and they would tell
me to go get another pail. I did go grudgingly, thinking
of devious ways to get revenge - revenge I never did get.
I couldn't hold it against my friends though, because

sometimes I too was one of the water bandits. When I finally managed to get home with the water my mother would give me a good smack for taking too long. I remember her smacking me and her arm hurting as a result because she had arthritis. I felt very sorry for my mom because she wouldn't hurt a fly. But along with the arthritis she also suffered with anxiety and terrible headaches because of her bad teeth. I can only imagine that sometimes it must just have been too much for her. I inherited these afflictions from my mom however, I was in a position to do something about them - she wasn't.

This soccer field - our park - was just an empty city block without houses and was located on the lower-numbered end of our street. Number one was the place where we listened to Radio Free Europe. It was also the place where another one of my good friends lived. He suffered for years spending untold hours on the violin. His name was Charles Honved (Patriot). His brother's name was Immy. Immy was exceptionally good with electronics and had all kinds of instruments, tools, resistors, tubes and switches. Had he been born later he might have become another Steve Jobs.

When my friends and I listened to the musical instruments on Radio Free Europe, we often discussed how we would have loved to learn to play the guitar, saxophone or piano - but couldn't afford them. All we had was Charles Honved, playing his violin in the afternoons while we were kicking a soccer ball around in front of his house. His father made him practice the violin every day and when he grew up he absolutely hated that instrument. He told us many times he wanted to 'kill his old man' but we knew he didn't really mean that. Had I been Charles' father, I would have realized how much my son hated the violin and not forced it on him. But I can't fault Mr. Honved. He and his wife didn't have much and only wanted Charles to stay away from bad influences, get an education and succeed in life. Charles went on to university and a few years later became the manager of a factory. But he never did learn to play that violin. When his father died, he may well have been unhappy that his son never even learned how to play *Mary Had a Little Lamb,* let alone the *Hungarian Rhapsody No. 2* by Franz Liszt.

~

Aside from soccer in the summer we also played a game called *Foot Tennis*. We could play this foot game with any rubber ball, just like the *heading* game, where you served and returned the ball with your head. This sort of high-energy activity could occupy two or four people at a time.

We also played *Rag Ball,* a different game that used an actual ball made of rags about the size of a loosely packed tennis ball. After we agreed on the goal markers we would slap the rag ball with the palm of our hand towards the goal. The game lasted for a set number of either six or twelve goals.

Another game we played was a very dangerous game called *Byge* (missile). We played this game without helmets or safety glasses and miraculously no one was killed. Our missile was made of wood. It was three centimetres round by six centimetres long and tapered at both ends. When this missile was flipped from its base and became airborne we would hit it back with a thin stick, similar to a baseball bat. Our opponent had to try to hit it while it was still in the air. If the missile fell to the ground our team advanced to that point and had another opening shot. The length of our playing field was the whole street. The winner was whoever advanced to the end of the street first. I once broke a neighbour's window with that missile. It was a double window and I only broke the outer glass. The neighbour never bothered fixing it, perhaps because he never knew it was broken. I would bet that window is the same way today as it was then.   ~

We played marbles a lot too, but with coloured clay balls. Real marbles were a rarity. One glass marble was worth ten clay balls. There were various games, the most popular being *Closest to the Line.* That game we also played with coins. From a set distance we had to

Honved, far left - me, far right.

flick a coin onto that line and whoever was on the line or closest to it, was the winner of all the previously thrown marbles or money. It definitely took accurate hand-eye coordination!

Button Football was the most popular game we played though. I liked this game because I was good at making the game pieces. I used overcoat buttons for defenders, jacket buttons for midfielders, and shirt buttons for balls. I collected brightly coloured cast off plastics to make layers which I glued together and shaped with files into little domes. My team colours were the same as the official soccer team colours.

To play this game we went to houses that had large laminate kitchen tables. The larger the table the better the game was. It is a shame *Button Football* never caught on in America. Brazilians used to come to Hungary to play matches, but we could never afford to travel to their country

~

In the park where we used to play, tiny brown mushrooms grew in patches and the whole neighbourhood feasted on them. However there were toadstools mixed in with these tame mushrooms and they were hard to tell apart. I could tell the difference and so could most locals. One day however Attila, who was seven years old at the time, came home with a good amount of mushrooms. My father checked them over and considered them to be okay. He cooked them up for supper with eggs and onions. After a few minutes he became so sick that he had to lie down. He knew right away what had happened. He had eaten a toadstool. I remember running to the corner store to phone for an ambulance. Within fifteen minutes my father was in the hospital. The doctor told us if my brother or I had eaten that toadstool we could have died. Attila and I were fine. We only had a slight stomach ache. My father had to have his stomach pumped. From that day forward we never let Attila pick the mushrooms again.

While that was a close call for me it wasn't anything compared to what happened one evening a week or so later. My friend Joe had his thirteen-year-old female cousin living at his house. An older kid from a local gang at school started to date her. Unbeknownst to us this kid thought we were hitting on his girlfriend. So he gathered up some of his gang members and headed to my house. I was so lucky Joe was at my place at the time. He was teaching me blackjack. My parents weren't home.

When we went to see who was ringing the doorbell, we found this gang of about ten tough guys tearing down our picket fence. The moment I stepped through the door someone hit me on the head with a slat from that fence. I went out like a light. I guess you could say they *rang my bell!* Joe in the meantime tried to tell them the girl was his cousin and I had nothing to do with her, I was merely a neighbour. They finally accepted Joe's explanation but not before cracking a few of his ribs and bloodying his nose. I must have gotten a concussion from that blow to my head. It left me with one terrible headache for several days.

Back then, same as today, it was a typical case of mistaken identity. I guess we were lucky they didn't have guns.

~

In Budapest according to a loosely written law one had to be sixteen years old to go to bars or hotels to consume alcohol. But in those days nobody gave a damn how old you were. My father or cousin Steve used to send me for a pitcher of beer when I was ten years old and on the way home I always took a gulp or two.

When I was fourteen my friend Joe was sixteen and we went everywhere together. In other words I started drinking when I was fourteen. No one cared because we weren't driving. We used the streetcars and we didn't purposely go out to get drunk. Drinking alcohol was incidental to me in those days.

Joe and I often went to a bar called *The Tulip*. It was in downtown Budapest near the street where I later went to technical school. The bar featured new bands, some of which equalled the most popular ones in the United States. These bands were allowed to play all the American songs on the hit parade. We learned many of them from the radio, mispronouncing the words because we didn't know what they meant. I still have some of those songs that I wrote down in an old notebook (including the misspellings). Come to think of it, and this is interesting to note, those bands were allowed to play capitalist music even though we were not allowed to listen to Radio Free Europe. Perhaps it was two separate things: music was art and Radio Free Europe was propaganda.

But we did listen to Radio Free Europe at Honved's place behind locked doors and in the evenings when the blinds were pulled down. That's where we heard of super sales in America -*buy a washing machine and get the dryer for a penny.* America was calling me and I was itching to go. Some ventured forth, some turned back, some didn't go at all and some unfortunately died trying to make it to the *Promised Land.*

~

One summer day I had a *major* incident at the local swimming pool, the Swan (*Hattyu.*) I spent most of the day playing in the shallow end where the water was warm and loaded with chlorine. As usual on my way out, I stopped at the Olympic pool and dipped my head into the cold water to slick back my hair. Somebody gave me a push and I went down to the bottom like an axe without a handle and stayed there. I lost consciousness instantly. Because I didn't surface, the person who pushed me or perhaps someone else dove in and rescued me. I saw no bright lights, angels, or God—*nothing*– I was dead as a doornail.

I don't want to sound repetitious, but when I came to once again, I was hanging upside down and puking water. After this *major* incident I decided to learn how to swim.

Chapter Twelve

I go dancing every Saturday. I befriend Steve Vegh. His sister is married to an attaché. I paint signs and make a little money. I have another friend in school who is a genius. I come close to dying again. I graduate from school and start my life of innovating.

Over the next few years I suffered a lot with bad teeth and lost at least one tooth per year. The pain from my teeth gave me headaches of biblical proportions. It seemed like I ate more aspirin than I did food. In 1951 during my first year in technical school my teeth ached so bad that it didn't matter whether I took aspirin, whisky, or gasoline—nothing helped. While riding my bicycle one time, a headache hit me so hard that I drove right into a fence bruising both my arms. These headaches continued until I was thirty years old and already living in Canada. I finally went and had all my remaining teeth removed—all fifteen of them—and have never had a headache since.

From 1951-55, bouts with my tooth-headaches aside, I was a pretty savvy teenager. I had better clothes than most others my age because I was the only one in my class with a steady part-time job. I was still painting communist slogans. With the money I earned, my mom used to buy me good used clothes at the flea market. Usually though, my parents used most of my earnings for necessities. Still we couldn't afford that hydro pole and I had to do my mechanical drawings by the light of a kerosene lamp.

Many of my after school hours were spent at Honved's house where we played a lot of cards, pinochle and chess and we went dancing every Saturday night. The admission was a few pennies and the dance lasted from nine in the evening until six in the morning. Because the streetcars didn't start up until six in the morning, it was customary to stay dancing all night.

~

I got to know Steve (*Pista, Vegh*) and we had many adventures together. One that I am not particularly proud of I remember it as if it happened yesterday. We were both earning money working. Steve worked in a machine shop and I at my part-time sign painting job.

One Sunday we decided to see how many bars we could visit before we got drunk. At each bar we order a half-litre of brown beer along with a shot of rum. We commonly called it a *boiler maker*. I think we managed to hit six bars. While we were walking home Steve lost his key and when we got to his house he couldn't get in. He started climbing over his picket fence and halfway up he fell backwards into a ditch. The ditch wasn't too deep so he didn't hurt himself. However, he didn't get up either. He fell asleep right then and there in the ditch. When his father went to work in the morning and saw him there, he didn't wake him up. Steve missed a day of work. I lived one street over and had a key stashed, thus had no problem getting into my house. The three litres of beer plus the six shots of rum we had was probably not a national record, but it was ours and we never repeated it.

~

A tragic event occurred in 1952 when I was already in technical school. I say this with deep sorrow. One of my schoolmates and soccer buddies Tibi (*Tyby)* died in the tank factory; the same factory where that boy played the piano and sang that memorable little song. Shortly after Tibi had finished grade eight he was so happy to have found work so close to home. I was happy for him too. But barely a month or two after he

92

was hired, the lifting magnet on the crane malfunctioned and dropped a steel plate on him, crushing him to death. I was shocked when I heard this devastating news. He was so young. I can still picture him to this day with his curly blond hair a subtle personality. He was just an all around nice kid and a good friend.

~

I must say I looked *cool* while attending technical school. I wore a wide-brimmed hat that was in style and always wore a tie in the fall and also sported some fancy scarves. I had two pairs of pants with alternating sports jackets and good shoes. A lady in the neighbourhood was a seamstress and I ordered two custom-made shirts from her. One of them was made from a fine black cloth.

I believe the way I dressed might have been the reason I never got high marks in technical school. I looked better than my teachers did. In those days kids that dressed in modern clothes were called *jampi,* meaning "flashy." The teachers were undoubtedly jealous because it was costly to dress that way. Those were the days when everybody in Hungary dressed their best when they went out to the city. Today that's all changed. They dress more casually now.

Charles, back row centre.

~

We were allowed to stay at the school to study after regular hours and those who paid a monthly fee could have a freshly cooked nutritious dinner. The Teacher's College next door shared the food with us. It was a real convenience.

An attractive young woman a couple years older than myself attended that Teacher's College and raced a *Moto Guzzi* professionally all over Europe. She parked her motor bike behind a locked wrought iron gate in front of the school. We were all thrilled to know such famous person. We re-told many of her interesting stories about races at the *Varos Liget* (City Park) or abroad. On the days she practised her racing, she wore a very sexy outfit of leather jacket and pants. That made all of us young guys walk on our tongues.

~

In my free time I played a lot of soccer, spent a lot of time studying, reading books and keeping busy with my stamp collection. I started collecting stamps when I was nine or ten and I had a fine array of stamps. It was a hobby that was easy on my pocket money and I was able to trade stamps with other kids, which was fun. I enjoyed the socialization and the building of friendships the hobby afforded me. My friends and I didn't care for drugs. If there were drugs in those days they were way out of our league. We didn't need drugs. The guys I hung out with were always high on life and I am still like that today. Other than reading about getting high on cocaine or marijuana, using them never entered our minds.

I always had a book in my hand even while I was walking. I read all the books in our neighbourhood library. I should have become a professor but my memory wasn't very good. Later in life I found out that my memory loss could have been caused by lead poisoning. The lead must have come from the water pipes or the paint on dinnerware or who knows where else. It had affected not only my brain but my nervous system as well. My legs quiver even today as I am sitting here. It feels like a thousand ants are crawling up and down them.

~

During the two month summer school break we were sent to various manufacturing plants where we could learn to operate machines or perform other shop related duties. We always looked forward to this inspiring event.

One year I was sent to a factory that made *screw machines* and I helped out in the assembling process. I made a pencilled copy of a screw machine and I still have that drawing today.

Another year I was sent to a textile factory where I had a chance to work on a real *lathe* in the maintenance department. That machine turned out to be the machine from hell.

I was given the night shift job of having to stop the machine frequently to measure the part that I was making.

On one of those occasions after I had turned the machine off, I was called away and forgot to take the chuck key out of the chuck. This particular key was made of steel and weighed about a half a kilogram and it looked like a 'T'.

When I came back to the lathe I had to bend down to start machine. The start button was at knee level. While straightening up I heard a whooshing sound and felt the air move above my head. In the next instant I heard glass breaking. It was a skylight near me that crashed to the floor. I probably said something like "*what the...*". I know I said something because the war was over and there were no bombs falling and nobody was shooting at me. Did a bird crash into the skylight? I wasn't sure. For several minutes I mulled over what might have happened and was dumbfounded. I couldn't come up with an answer.

I kept the machine running and finished the final cut on the part I was so meticulously making. Then I reached for the chuck key, and it wasn't in its usual place. Suddenly I broke out in a cold sweat... The breeze and the whooshing sound had actually been made by the chuck key flying above my head at demonic speed. Had I been quicker at standing up... I shudder to think what might have happened. I could have died!

Now how was I supposed to open the chuck without a key? It was impossible. From the gaping hole in the skylight I could see the direction the key took. All

I had to do was go outside and find it in the yard. I remember it was a full moon and I looked for that chuck key until it was time to go home in the morning. At home I thought about the centrifugal force that we all learned about in school the month before.

The next day I went in early and looked for the key some more and I never did find it. Since I was the only operator on that machine on that particular night shift, I requisitioned another chuck key from the tool crib and nobody was ever the wiser. This was a *minor* event but could have been *major* as that chuck key could have been the first rocket to the moon.

Dire lesson learned; never leave a key in the machine chuck.

~

While I was good at painting communist slogans using basic tools; I really didn't do anything outstanding or important until after I finished technical school when I began innovating on everything.

In my final year we all had to choose a shop project and I decided to make a favorite item fashioned out of metal; a T-34 Russian tank. Not a real one, just an imitation model. I got top marks for it and I am pretty proud of it even today.

~

I should have mentioned this remarkable technical school buddy of mine earlier, but I wanted to keep him for *the icing on the cake.* Imre Mate was an extraordinary individual. He could read an entire book - of any size - in about ten minutes and had the ability to remember the contents by page number. He never kept notes in school and he never did homework. All the teachers knew he was exceptional and I don't think they even bothered to grade him. Imre passed all the subjects with the highest possible marks.

For some reason he only chummed around with

me. Perhaps he thought I was special too or maybe he just liked me because I respected him.

Almost every day during the noon break we would go for a walk and explore different parts of Budapest. He would do most of the talking and I would do the listening. I wish I could remember half the things he told me. He was weird in a fascinating kind of way. He had an amazingly vivid imagination. He talked about the future and how technology would evolve. He talked about life on other planets and even about people living in undiscovered jungles...he talked about so many interesting things...

One unusual incident with Imre in particular sticks out in my mind. We would light a cigarette and head down the street towards the Gellert Hotel, a five-star establishment with a swimming pool and spa. Its waters were rumoured to have healing powers. He started telling me about the history of this special bath house and hotel and I listened to him in total amazement wondering how he could know all this. We often went on walks like this and would then return to class. But this walk was different. After this, he just wasn't around anymore.

We lost contact with one another and I had no idea what became of him until one evening while I was playing cards at Honved's house, listening to Radio Free Europe. The radio announced that Imre and six others had hijacked a passenger plane to Vienna, Austria. Put that in your pipe and smoke it I said to myself. I could only shake my head. How amazing.

~

As to the Gellert Hotel, I almost drowned there once too. I was maybe thirteen or fourteen at the time. The pool had a wave machine that cycled every quarter of an hour. One day while I happened to be in the deep end, the cycle started. In order to stay above the waves, people would stretch out their arms at shoulder level flapping them like flightless birds. Unaware, they were pushing me down every time a wave rolled in. I couldn't stay above water long enough to avoid swallowing water. I don't remember whether I could swim by then or not but it wouldn't have made any difference because there were wall-to-wall people in the pool. Luckily for me the waves were going towards the shallow end and somehow I drifted to safety.

~

At the same age I had another scary experience at the Gellert swimming pool. I was splashing around possibly trying to learn to swim when a man approached me and started talking to me. He looked to be around thirty years old. He started to toss me into the air and was asking me if I liked to be tossed. Of course I liked it! It was fun to be thrown up into the air and to fall splashing back into the water. But I began to get this strange feeling... every time he lifted me up he had his hand on my genitals. I didn't over-think it at the time though because in order to throw me into the air he had to push me up by my bum.

As we chatted he honed in about my stamp collecting and that got my attention. He was no novice - he knew what strings to pull and I fell right into his trap. He said he had an album with him in his cabin locker which was located behind the pool area. He told me he would be most pleased if he could show it to me. In fact he added, if I would come to his house he would show me all his albums, all the while hinting that he was some famous collector. He mentioned his name, then he asked for mine. He talked about stamps with such enthusiasm that I was infatuated and elated. I felt so lucky to have met such a person - a stamp collector just like me. I thought perhaps he would give me some stamps I didn't already have. I was crazy about triangular and odd-shaped stamps.

I was too young and not yet capable of fully rationalizing this situation. In my mind I was thinking that if he gave me stamps I would have to give him something in exchange and I didn't have my collection with me. I contemplated over what I could give him in return and mentioned this to him. He told me not to worry and that he would give me stamps that he had multiples of. Once we got to his house, he would put them in an envelope for me. At the time, my mind was reasoning that giving away only the stamps you have multiples of made sense, yet I felt uncomfortable.

He told me he would come with me to get my clothes from my locker and that I could change at his cabin. I still heard no major warning bells ringing. My mind was mush thinking of fabulous collections and important stamps I didn't yet have.

I blindly followed him back to his cabin, *I had no fear.* Once there, I started taking off my bathing suit. It was wet and stuck to my body. He approached me and said he could help. Still I didn't clue in. As he pulled my bathing suit off he fondled my penis and scrotum and this scared me to death! I immediately pushed him away, pulled my pants on, picked up the rest of my clothes and ran like hell from that cabin. The man was calling my name and even attempted to catch me but I made it into the hotel lobby and instantly felt safe. People were staring at me, but because I was just a kid they were not concerned that I was getting dressed in the lobby. I never went to the Gellert alone again; at least not until I was old enough to take care of myself.

~

When I graduated from Technical School I wasn't too pleased with the marks I had received. I knew my school work had been better than what those grades implied. I was always self-confident and accomplished any task the school threw at me. I participated in all the extracurricular activities. I took drama, sang in the school choir, was a good gymnast, played soccer and was popular amongst my peers.

My first chance to show what I could really do came with my first real job.

The school assisted students in finding their first employment and I got a job at *Muszaki Muvek* (Special Technologies) as a quality control employee. My department made pressed metal parts such as metal dishes, toys and light bulb ends etc.

Being an innovator from an early age quickly began to pay off. Within six months I was promoted to foreman. By then I already had several innovations. For these I was paid handsomely. I received money for years, even after I came to Canada. In order to avoid paying me for any future innovations, the company made me the superintendent, a position that included all manufacturing improvements.

My shop consisted of several trades; electricians, millwrights and thirty-seven female workers. Some of these women had just arrived from North Korea. They were like beautiful flowers in a garden of Eden. I was constantly in love with almost every one of them. They were all between the ages of eighteen and thirty and I felt like a rabbit guarding carrots.

However I was told, even threatened not to fraternize with the female employees. Being a company person I understood the ramifications and tried to comply but I have to admit I failed terribly. I cannot blame myself for being a normal young guy.

Like any healthy male, on my own time, I took them dancing, hiking, swimming or even camping. The fact that I was drawn to lovely women validated that I was quite normal. My fraternizing didn't disclose any company secrets because there weren't any. And I wasn't a spy.

A particular incident comes to mind. I was called into the office again to have another conversation with the plant manager about the women in the shop. I thought perhaps he was either just too old or too oblivious to the opposite sex. I told him not to worry about me. I had a girlfriend from somewhere else. Less than a week later while my girlfriend and I were at a popular vacation spot, I had to look twice to believe my eyes. There was my plant manager with a young woman from the shop! The proverb *'do as I say, not as I do'* came to mind.

Because I left Hungary shortly after my promotion no one will ever know if I would have been fired or would have died of exhaustion due to all my extracurricular activities!

Chapter Thirteen

Budapest, Yugoslavia, Canada.
Hungary revolts against the Russians. (What took us so long)?
I decide to leave my homeland. I escape to Yugoslavia and wind up in a WWII concentration camp. I already feel free.

M y sister Aniko, was born February 7, 1956 and my parents were thrilled. They had always wanted a girl.

In October of 1956 the revolution started and ended in just a few days. The factory where I worked was right next door to a military barracks which was a very dangerous place.

Tanks crowded the street in front of my factory.

I was probably the last person to get home by streetcar as no more streetcars were coming from that part of Budapest. Once again Hungary faced terrible times and many good men and women lost their lives. I could have lost my life too because the revolution was brutal. The Russians came in with tanks and shot at people with cannons. Many volumes have been written about the Freedom Fighters and their achievements, gains and losses, so I will not repeat them. I learned later from my parents that the AVO had been looking for me. They detained anyone they thought might have been associated with the revolution, but by then I had left the country.

During the uprising I lost some of my buddies. Others like me, left with the hope of finding a better life in the West. My friend Joe Vinklar stayed back and did all right for himself. He couldn't flee anyway because he was in the army. I would have found myself in the army too had I stayed. I would have served in the artillery. They had no idea how much I already knew about artillery shells.

I didn't leave Hungary until January 19, 1957 months after the uprising had failed. My journey to freedom was tough but not insurmountable. I kept a personal diary of my unpleasant days as well as the days I cherished.

Steven (Vegh Pista) with my little sister.

My family wished me well on my departure. After bidding my mother, little sister and brother goodbye, my father and I left the house. I had asked my brother Attila to come with me but he had declined. There was an eight year age difference between us and he was in an entirely different world. When we were small I used to 'torture' him by bugging and tickling him until he cried. My parents would discipline with me for that! But as we grew up there was a mutual understanding between us, enough for me to extend the invitation for him to accompany me. There were no hard feelings when he chose to stay in Hungary.

My father and I walked to the streetcar and I kissed him goodbye when he got off at his workplace. I continued on to the train station. I certainly looked the part of a refugee. I wore my shabbiest pants, shirt, jacket and overcoat. It didn't matter because I was heading to America the *Land of Plenty.* I figured I could buy the best of everything once I got there.

I was full of fear and apprehension because I desperately wanted to avoid getting caught at the border. Miraculously, I never encountered any police patrols or border guards throughout my journey to Yugoslavia.

~

I travelled from Budapest with a buddy who had worked in the same factory as me albeit in a different area. Once we got off the slow-moving train which had decelerated to let people off; I picked out a bright star to follow and we headed in that direction. It turned out to be a good choice. We walked over fields for about two hours, roughly eight kilometres and did not see any houses until we were close to the border. Near the border, we asked for directions from a local farmer and he assured us we were on the right track. We gave him a lot of Hungarian *Forints* for a bottle of his moonshine because he said *Forints* were no good in Yugoslavia and he was right. Two other young chaps tagged along as we made our way across the undefended border.

It was a wintery night but not too cold and the two chaps each had a bottle of whiskey to keep them warm. The border was not guarded because Hungary's communist government had more important and nefarious things to worry about than a bunch of idiots trying to escape from one communist country into another. Yugoslavia was a communist regime and we had no idea what would happen to us once we got there.

As it turned out, I had made the right decision by choosing to go through Yugoslavia even though it was a communist country. *Tito* had his own version of communism. Perhaps he received financial support from the West and turned a blind eye to escaping Hungarians. In the end we all made it to our freedom.

Upon arriving in Yugoslavia, we were carted to various cities from the Hungarian collection points. I will always be grateful to those people who helped us. On January 25, 1957 we were taken to Gerovo. This was a former German concentration camp complete with a double barbed wire fence with a walkway between the wires and a lookout tower in each corner. However we didn't feel like prisoners because we knew it was only a matter of time before we would be on our way to the *Promised Land.*

I said goodbye to the two fellows that had joined us at the border. They were homesick and had decided to return to Hungary. I was never homesick. I was determined to settle somewhere other than Hungary. Anywhere, even in Europe would have done it, but my preference was the United States. The country I believed to be the land of opportunity.

Camp Gerovo was no Hilton. We slept on straw mattresses in double or triple-stacked bunk beds. Everyone had one enamelled bowl from which to eat. We only had cold water. Just imagine washing your dish in cold water let alone taking a shower, especially in the winter? I thought about Yany in Siberia.

In the mornings we were given coffee made from burned barley along with a piece of bread. The coffee looked like mud. They served us some sort of greasy food for lunch; pork and beans if we were lucky. The quality of the food was pretty poor but it was edible. The bread was like play dough and we made chess figures out of it. We took turns working in the kitchen peeling large heaps of potatoes with knives that couldn't even cut butter.

A care package arrived once from the Red Cross. It contained toothbrushes, tubes of toothpaste, shaving brushes and shaving soap that didn't foam at all in cold water. I still have that cone-shaped soap. It's probably fossilized by now. The Red Cross also sent used clothes but the Yugoslavian soldiers took the best items for themselves. We were left with rags and worn out shoes and rubber boots with holes in them - probably the cast-offs from the soldiers. I remember ripping my bed sheet into triangles and fashioning these into underwear. We had no access to medical care either and couldn't even get an Aspirin. At times my aching teeth damn near killed me.

One of my roommates was a very personable chap about ten years my senior. He was an engraver and for a couple of cigarettes he would cut your name into a lighter or a watch -anything made of metal. Fifty years later he became one of my most important characters in my book, *The Passengers.*

I spent five months at that camp under extremely substandard conditions. A lot of people complained about life there and I could have complained too but I was looking at the brighter side of things. I was happy to have had made it this far alive! I was happy then and am happy now.

Nothing could have been worse than the times I spent on cold winter nights in Budapest standing in the bakery line wearing nothing but rags and freezing my toes off.

I never felt so alone than amongst those masses of destitute people who talked to each other but seldom said anything to a child. There were other young children ahead of me and behind me. We could not leave our place in the line. This was a very strict rule; must remain in line two-by-two. I learned that rule at an early age. Everyone was in rags and feeling just as famished and lonely as myself. Of this I am certain.

During those years I had sensed there was something wrong with our government but I couldn't do anything about it. I had a vague idea about America and what it stood for - *freedom*. I also knew what the Russians stood for – communism - a utopian idea that has never worked and never will.

In Gerovo some men couldn't bear the living conditions and tried to escape. I often wondered where they thought they were escaping to. We were about three thousand metres above sea level, in ancient mountains with only a single-lane road leading in and out of that camp plus it was the middle of winter. Those that did try to escape were caught and brought back and were punished. Some tried to escape a second time and they would once again be brought back. Second-time escapees would be put into a barren hole in the ground. We could hear them screaming day after day. Imagine being in an earthen hole in the winter with nothing but a couple of potato sacks to lie on. I don't know what happened to those guys and could never understand why they wanted to 'escape'. They could easily have died of pneumonia and I am sure some of them probably did.

~

In early 1957 a Canadian representative came to the camp and I signed up to go to Canada. The United States quota had already been filled. Through correspondence with my parents I learned that Mrs. Amelia Gabriel née Balatoni, my former babysitter was living in Brantford, Ontario and she would take me in until I found a job. Even though things were looking pretty good for me I was anxious. Time ticked away into spring and we were having nice weather. The harsh winter was behind us. We even played soccer in March without shirts as we waited our turn to leave the camp. In May of 1957 my deliverance from Gerovo arrived.

The big day was finally here and we, the *Canadians,* left the camp in covered trucks on the 17th of May. The next day we arrived at the resort town of Rijeka, Yugoslavia, by the Adriatic coast. We stayed in a lovely hotel for a few days. I went swimming and felt like a crustacean from all the salt on my body. That was the first time I ever swam in the sea and I thought of it as a big deal. And, just imagine sleeping in a beautiful clean bed. That was an even bigger deal!

I'll never forget the intoxicating fragrance of the blossoming olive trees in Rijeka or the fishermen in the evenings as they fished from tiny boats with carbide lamps. Music resonated from a local bar. What a romantic place it was. I have always wanted to return there for a visit.

When *Tito* died, everything fell apart. The country split into seven different nations. It reminds me of the saying; *united we prosper, divided we fall.* I wrote some descriptive poetry about Yugoslavia's break-up under the pretence that I had a brother there and addressed my letters of dismay to him.

We left Rijeka by train travelling through dozens of tunnels in Italy and Switzerland. On May 27, 1957 we arrived in Le Havre, France, where we boarded the

Italian ship, the *Ascania*.

On May 30, after waiting in port for three days, we finally set sail. I immediately became seasick. However, by the end of our uneventful voyage I was cured. The most interesting sight for me, as we sailed down the St. Lawrence River, was seeing enormous floating icebergs.

We had each been given five Canadian dollars as spending money on board the ship and when we disembarked in Québec City on June 6, 1957 we were given another five dollars. This money didn't last very long. In other words I came to Canada with nothing. I couldn't even speak English. A day later, I arrived in Brantford, Ontario.

~

Travelling by train from Québec City to Brantford was an incredible experience. Nothing could have been more exhilarating or more interesting to me than the big automobiles on wide highways. The large houses, the huge new looking cities and the great open spaces between towns was all too much for me to take in. Canada appeared to be shiny and new. In comparison my homeland Hungary, and the rest of post-war Europe, looked grey and used up, with buildings and land devastated by wars.

I was speechless, so to speak.

Kid Without Fear

Charles Eric Jambor

Part Two

Canada

Chapter Fourteen

Brantford is a pretty cool city. My uncle *Alex comes to visit me. I am learning English. I have a major death-defeating event. I set my **foot** in the USA.*

After I arrived at the train station in Brantford, Ontario, I was in a state of euphoria. Everything I saw, tasted or touched was different, new and pleasant. I savoured every sensation until I wore it out. I must say my euphoria has never worn off. These emotions are just as special to me today as they were then. I felt my future was starting here and I couldn't wait to revel in it.

~

Mrs. Gabriel (*Milikeneni*) greeted me at the Brantford train station. I remember the last time I saw her was in the late 1940s when she came to our house to see my parents, to say goodbye. As I understood it, she was leaving the country. She brought her two girls. Kati was just a baby all bundled up and sleeping in the rear seat of a bicycle and Susan was a little older and already walking. We lived on *Barcsay* Street at this time and only my mom and I were home. I didn't know much about emigration to another country therefore didn't give it another thought. It is remarkable how a decade later and thousands of kilometres apart we meet again.

Since her husband was a military man and was away a lot, I barely remember him. All I know is that he was a tall heavy set, burly man.

When I arrived at Mrs. Gabriel's house in Cainsville (just south of Brantford) I was feeling elated. She turned on the TV for me and I think 'Howdy Doody' was on. I must have been a strange sight for her two girls because I couldn't speak English, was oddly dressed and did not understand what was being said on TV.

Within a day or so, Mrs. Gabriel drove me out to a farm where I accepted a job as a hired man.

Remember, I had been raised in the big city. I didn't even know which end of a cow to milk despite having watched my cousin milk cows on a few occasions back in the vineyards. I had seen horses, pigs, chickens and turkeys as well, but I really didn't know what to do with any of them. I was thinking; *what the hell is a guy with a mechanical school diploma going to do on a farm anyway*? I found out fast.

Mrs. Gabriel gave me an ancient Hungarian-English dictionary and I started learning English eagerly. I watched television knowing it would help me with the language even though I didn't understand a word at the time.

For the first few days I walked the couple of kilometres back and forth between the farm and Mrs. Gabriel's until the farmer Ernie, suggested I get my stuff and move over to his place. "To save time!" he said.

However, the time saved was more beneficial to Ernie than to me because now I could get up really early to milk the cows, gather the eggs, drive the tractor, clean the barn and the pigsty, mow the grass, etc. My pay was fifty dollars a month! At first that seemed like a lot of money to me, but actually it was only enough for cigarettes and a small gift package that I would send to my parents in Hungary. Once I sent a big doll for my little sister. I think she still has that doll today.

~

While at the farm, I got a letter from my dad telling me about his American cousin Alex Yambor who lived in Akron, Ohio. After I found out how to make a long distance call to the USA I phoned him and he was very excited to hear from me. He promised to come and see me in a few weeks. I was overjoyed and could hardly wait for his visit. He wasn't a real *uncle* but that's what I called him.

Uncle Alex came with his wife Pearl, his sister Teresa and her husband Jack. They took me to Niagara Falls where uncle Alex wined and dined me and gave me some American dollars. Not one of them spoke good Hungarian and Jack not at all because he was American. However, we managed to get along just fine. My uncle promised to get me into the United States lickety-split and said he was going to send me the immigration papers right away. The USA had originally been my destination choice. I could hardly wait.

To clarify, I'd like to briefly describe the family dynamics. My father's dad was Frank and Alex's dad was Bill.

Frank and Bill were brothers. They came to America around 1905.   After working for a few years Frank returned to Hungary with some money he'd made and purchased the property where my father was later born. Dad's siblings were Julia, Steven, Joe, and Paul. They were older than my dad by at least ten years and had all been born before Frank left for America. Frank remained in Hungary.

Bill stayed in the USA and brought out his wife and children. I never knew Bill or his wife but knew his kids; Teresa, Joe, Mary, Alex(uncle) and Lou, who was born in the USA.

Teresa never had children. Joe had one daughter Irene. Mary had one daughter, Jerry. Alex had one son

Alex Jr. Lou I never met but I understand he had children.

Uncle Alex was known as 'Sr.' and his son as 'Jr.'

My family related mostly to Joe's daughter *aunt* Irene, with her husband William (Willy) Kovacs; and to Alex Yambor Jr. with his wife Betty. Our families often visited each other.

After the two brothers arrived in the USA, Bill had wanted to have his family name pronounced with a 'Y' to keep it phonetically correct - hence Yambor not Jambor. By the way, Jambor in Hungarian means gentle, pious, and honourable. I blush every time someone asks if there is a meaning to my name. With a name like that I should have been a politician. (Honestly?)

~

I checked the mailbox every day, anxiously awaiting the papers from uncle Alex.

I was learning English as I was driving the farm tractor. I had put words on pieces of paper the night before. Luckily for me there was a retired schoolteacher on the next farm, Mrs. Stone. She was kind and patient enough to teach me the language and helped me put my new words into sentences. I appreciated that greatly. I wish she was still around to see what I have done with those words. Mrs. Stone had nice daughter Edith who had a best friend named Lorraine. Those two names appealed to me so much that I've used them in my books time and time again.

~

Ernie, the farmer was a good head and we got along just fine. He loved fancy cars. He had a brand new Chrysler that had to be pulled by tractor in the winter to get it started. The door locks on this car also froze shut all the time. I don't know how he put up with that vehicle.

~

One stormy morning the cows were already lining up at the gate to be milked. They found their stanchions in the barn and I was about to attach the milking machine to one of them when lightning struck the building. I was knocked out and don't remember what happened. When I awoke, I was in bed and a doctor was asking me questions I didn't understand. He was smiling. That told me I must be okay. The incident was reported in the *Brantford Expositor.* Ernie's wife Doris, cut it out for me and I kept that article for years. It's still be around somewhere.

~

That winter I built a snowman or I should say a snow woman. This snow sculpture was so elegant that it too made the paper. I have a photo of it.

I also went skating with Edith Stone on a mud run that was opposite Ernie's farm and learned a few more thousand words. I never dated Edith or Lorraine because I couldn't afford a girlfriend and still needed to learn more English.

Snow woman.

Finally a letter arrived from uncle Alex with some forms that needed to be filled out which I did, and sent them back to him. In a few weeks I received more documents and another letter from my uncle telling me that once these new papers were completed I could come to the United States. We would discuss the date later by phone. My destination choice, the USA, was actually going to happen.

This was in the spring of 1958 and with my paperwork in hand, I said goodbye to Ernie.
He took me to the bus depot in Brantford where I bought a ticket for Akron, Ohio.

As the bus drove over the bridge towards the United States, I saw the American flag and broke out in goosebumps saying a silent, *all right!* I started having grandiose visions about achieving great goals, getting married and having kids.

The bus stopped on the American side of the Peace Bridge and a customs officer came aboard and started checking documents. I was sitting alone in the third row grinning at the officer, waiting for him to grin back. He didn't.

When he got to me he asked me for my passport. I had all my papers ready and turned them over to him. He took a little while to examine everything and I began to worry there was something wrong. Finally, he handed them back and told me they were incomplete and I had to get off the bus. I almost fainted. In broken English I asked him what I was supposed to do now. He told me I had to go back to Canada.

"How?" I asked.

He said I had to walk back across the bridge.

I scampered off the bus with my travel bag and started walking. While gazing down at Niagara River, I am certain that if I could have seen my reflection in the water it would have shown the image of the most miserable person in the whole wide world.

Upon arriving back to Canada Customs, at the other end of the bridge, an officer asked me for my passport. I handed him my papers and tried to explain what had happened. He told me I didn't have the proper papers and couldn't enter Canada.

I was dumbfounded. It took me a few minutes to figure out my next move. I had my 'Landed Immigration' paper from the ship *Ascania* and gave him that too. By this time other officers had joined in and they were all talking amongst themselves. I hardly understood a word. Some appeared to be snickering. They told me I had to stay on the bridge! At that point it dawned on me that they were just having fun. Once they'd had their laughs, they let me go and directed me to the bus depot where I purchased a ticket to Toronto. I stayed in a hotel overnight and bought a ticket to Brantford the next day. From the bus depot I hitch hiked a ride back to Ernie's place. Needless to say Ernie was shocked. *Happy?* that I had returned!

When I called uncle Alex and told him what had happened he couldn't believe it. He said he would fix the situation. However, nothing happened for months and I finally gave up waiting. I found out later that his wife had left him and assumed that was why he never got back to me.

Over the next few years whenever anyone asked me if I had been to the United States, I would tell them yes, I had set my *foot* onto the US side of the Peace Bridge. They naturally always thought I was joking. This escapade, surprisingly didn't affect me much for very long. Canada was just fine with me.

~

Besides having dairy cows Ernie also grew strawberries. He asked me one day if I could paint berries, his name and his address on both sides of his truck. I did the job and he liked my work very much. His business became recognizable to everyone.

During the strawberry season he would employ a lot of pickers and from time to time he would drive them to more distant fields that he rented from other farmers all over the county. He loaded the pickers onto his truck and drove them to those locations.

One day while we were driving to a nearby field we took an elderly strawberry picker along with us. The man sat in the back of the truck on a bench where Ernie could keep an eye on him through the rear-view mirror. Everything was fine until Ernie had just passed an intersection. Suddenly he didn't see the man anymore. He immediately stopped and we ran back to that intersection. There was the poor fellow on the side of the road, lifeless. A nearby resident had seen him fall off the truck and had rushed to him with a blanket. We found out later that he'd had a heart attack.

Chapter Fifteen

I have played cards all my life but the stakes were never high. To me cards are the same everywhere only the faces are different. I sing in a band. We race cars on the Grand River.

It didn't take me long to find a card game in Brantford. We'd get into a car and go to someone's house where we would play Twenty-One or Dealer's Choice poker. I don't recall ever losing much money at playing cards but I remember vividly winning big time in a crap game at the Onondaga Fire Hall. The guys I played with, knew me and they knew I was *hot*. That evening I won over three hundred dollars, six month's wages! My parents were happy because I sent them a hundred dollars. They could finally buy that hydro pole and get power into their house.

In my letters I told them that I was a 'cowboy'. In Hungary this was a status symbol. It would have been a 'status' for me too had I owned a ranch. In any case, they were mystified and that was enough for me.

Sometimes my friends and I went to one of the famous hotels in Brantford; the Graham Bell, Bodega, Alexander or the Kirby. There was always a game going on upstairs, in a private room. But there, you had to have big money. Usually I just watched. I saw guys win and I saw guys lose. I heard stories about gamblers losing a house or a farm and I heard how some committed suicide over a major loss. Fights were common. Those kinds of gamblers were out of my league.

One night after leaving the Kirby hotel, I almost

walked into a fist fight. A fellow had his back against a brick wall and in the split second before he was about to be punched in the face, he moved his head sideways and the aggressor slammed his fist into that brick wall. I had never seen anything like this in my life. The knuckles on his left hand were driven back and probably broken. I remember hoping that he was right-handed.

~

On Sunday my routine was to go to the Blue Haven restaurant in Cainsville to play the pinball machine and have my favourite western sandwich. Mrs. Minken, the owner was Ukrainian and an awesome cook. We got along extremely well perhaps because I still knew some Russian words and the Russian language is very close to Ukrainian. It appeared to me though, that she didn't want anything to do with Russians. I'm unsure as to why exactly, but I assume it might have had something to do with Stalin's starvation of the Ukrainian people in 1916.

She had two sons, Murray and Fred and both were older than I. Neither owned a car. The younger one, Murray, used to hitchhike into Brantford for entertainment. In the evening a Blue Haven customer would pick him up and bring him home or I would, if I saw him. Often though, he stayed in a Brantford hotel overnight. Murray and Fred took turns waiting on tables at the Blue Haven.

Eating cabbage rolls at the Blue Haven was a regular event especially when I was working at a factory and still single. Mrs. Minken's cabbage rolls were delicious. My grandmother's sauerkraut came to mind. I eventually learned to make cabbage rolls myself and I think mine were just as good. I also learned to make stuffed peppers. Maybe some chefs in Hungary can make them better but I don't know anyone around my neighbourhood that can!

Fred passed away at an early age and shortly after that his parents died. Eventually Murray - who was also getting on in years - found a lovely woman and got married.

~

I could hardly wait for the weekends. Various bands would play at the Blue Haven on Saturdays. In my broken English, I would sing along with the musicians. Some people though my singing was pretty good. Everyone thought I was French. I didn't think I was that good; but look at Johnny Cash, people in those days thought he couldn't sing either. It was all quite funny to me. Learning country music and singing it without knowing exactly what the words meant was quite amusing.

~

One evening while sitting in the restaurant, a young man in a frantic state came rushing in. This man told us that he and two of his friends had been hitchhiking opposite the restaurant when a vehicle hit all three of them. He said his friends had been killed. Mrs. Minken called the police immediately and we rushed out to see if we could help.

The two young men were indeed dead and the vehicle hadn't stopped. Those poor fellows never knew what hit them. For years afterwards and even to this day, whenever I drive past that spot, I look. I don't know what I'm looking for—certainly not for the people that perished there that fateful night. Maybe I'm looking for ghosts?

~

On another evening, again while sitting with my friends at the Blue Haven, we heard a crash. It sounded like an explosion further down on Hwy 2 at the bridge over Fairchild Creek. We rushed out and looked towards the bridge. A car had hit the concrete bridge structure so hard that there were still car parts sliding and spinning on the highway. We ran to help but there was nothing we could do. When the fire truck arrived we could still hear moans coming from the unrecognizable wreck. but the person died before they could get him out. The police said the man had been inebriated and had fallen asleep at the wheel.

Our friend Hank Misters died in the same manner. He was one of our card playing buddies. Hank was a mailman. He too was a heavy drinker. He would get intoxicated every weekend and sometimes even during the week. One Friday night as he was driving home from work on that same highway, he fell asleep at the wheel and crossed over into the other lane, hitting a young couple head-on. They regrettably, were badly hurt. Hank was killed. I still have the pictures that we took of his demolished car.

I've always felt that drinking and driving don't mix.

~

The following spring I bought a Norton motorbike. It was an English war bike. I'd love to still have it today, but it didn't turn out that way. In the summer of 1958 a young fellow named Keith Nelson moved in with Ernie and me. He borrowed my bike and took it out onto the gravel road. He said he knew how to handle a motorbike. He had no shirt or helmet on and I guessed he was going to show off his driving skills in front of Edith Stone and her friend Lorraine. They had just returned home from church and were chatting by the roadside. Keith increased his speed and lost control of the bike as he got near the girls and side-swiped them, tearing off their skirts. He went cart-wheeling into the ditch, shredding his rubber boots to pieces and tearing patches of skin off of his back and face. Luckily neither one of the girls was hurt. This incident must have been extremely painful for him, but what happened later in the afternoon was almost tragic for me.

Ernie took Keith to the hospital while I tended to my motorbike. I was in the middle of the yard picking shredded petticoat fabric from the spokes and gears when I heard thunder. It certainly looked like rain. As I was pushing the bike to a nearby shed one huge bolt of lightning cracked and knocked me off my feet. I must have been lying on the ground beside my motorbike for quite a while because when I came to, Ernie and Keith were just returning from the hospital. Because I had been wearing rubber boots and hanging onto rubber handle grips I didn't get the full force of the lightning strike. I was knocked out cold but luckily, other than a major headache, I was unhurt. After that I didn't know where to hang out or hide when a storm came!

Later I took the transmission on my motorbike apart and found a broken gear. I bought a new one and reassembled everything and the bike ran like new. I even bragged to my parents in a letter about how I was herding cows with my motorbike and pulling hay wagons with it too. That powerful bike saw its final day later that same year.

~

I bought my first car, a 1950 Studebaker, paid two hundred dollars for it and that took me two years to pay off. Once I had four wheels I travelled by car everywhere and got to know a wider circle of friends.

The winter of 1958 was so cold that the Grand River froze over. We could race our cars on it between Onondaga and Cayuga. It was a thrill to speed at sixty to eighty kilometres an hour then slam on the brakes. The car would spin out of control and rotate around four or five times before it would hit a snow bank and stop.

On Hwy 54 between Onondaga and Middleton,

there was a boat launch where we used to launch our cars onto the ice from. By the time I joined in on the fun there were already many others racing up and down the frozen river. In those days one could buy snow tires with studs that helped the cars to go faster on the ice, up to a hundred, maybe even a hundred and twenty kilometres per hour. The guys driving those cars must have known what they were doing because none of them ever rolled over or crashed. We certainly got out of their way in a hurry! It was fascinating to watch cars racing on the Grand River where we used to watch boats racing in the summer.

~

I quit working for Ernie that year but not before I was hit by lightning once again. It happened during the evening milking time. When the lightning hit the barn I fell to the floor. The last thing I heard was the rattling sound of the stanchions as the cows jumped from the jolt. Eventually someone found me and once again I was okay - obviously, because I am here today.

After I left Ernie's farm, to my knowledge, the barn was never hit by lightning again and apparently it had never been hit before I arrived either. The barn is still standing there at R.R. #1, Brantford, Ontario.

The barn has always had a lightning rod.

Chapter Sixteen

Swine can outrun cheetahs. I get a job many people wouldn't do. It occurs to me that I am not too smart after all, might even be dumb. I am lucky twice. I become skilful with a jackhammer.

D onny Harris was another one of the chaps I used to hang around with. When I was between jobs I lived at his place. Donny's farm was about half a kilometre from Ernie's. Donny was just as crazy as me and our other friends, maybe a tad crazier. He thought nothing of mixing deadly chemicals with his bare hands before spraying his corn. He'd take a plugged spray nozzle and blow it out with his mouth. That was the ultimate crazy. If Donny were around today it would be a miracle, and his life should be recorded in a book of chemistry.

Donny used to drive a car with no brakes. When we were together and he wanted to stop, it was my job to lean hard on a 2x4 piece of wood stuck through the floor. I remember this because we had to stop once to relieve ourselves by the road and I struggled with that 2x4. We were dribbling along merrily when a bird - possibly an owl - flew up from the ditch and scared the heck out of us, causing us to spray all over each other's legs.

~

When I left Donny's I went to work for another farmer by the name of George Markle. He had milking cows and raised pigs in a huge sty. Besides farming, George did plumbing and straightened barns. One of my jobs was to shovel out the liquid manure that at times was thirty to forty centimetres deep. This had to be done every week. There was a small opening in the rear barn wall, the size of a regular basement window. I shovelled the sludge out through this opening using a big aluminum shovel. Once in a while I missed and the liquid splashed back into my face. Not too many people - maybe Mike Rowe on TV's *Dirtiest Jobs* - would ever have done this kind of work. I did do it though because I was never afraid of work. Any work. Before George hired me, he did that job himself. As far I was concerned it wasn't a big deal, it was just a job that had to be done.

One day in the winter, the pigs broke out of the sty. Somehow I managed to get all two hundred of them back in with the exception of one. This particular animal ran away every time I went near it. I even tried to lasso it but nothing slowed this wild swine down. When I chased it, it ran behind the sty and somehow managed to scramble over the half metre deep manure.
I sank down into it. I couldn't help but think of my father being trapped in that sewage ditch during the air raid in Budapest. My rubber boots were stuck so I stepped out of them and chased that porker in my bare feet. The pig eventually collapsed from exhaustion and I almost did too. When I dragged it back to the sty the other pigs ate it.

By now I was making one hundred and twenty-five dollars a month! I was learning some interesting barn straightening tricks but most importantly I learned a lot about the plumbing trade, something I dabble in even today. However I never straightened any barns.

~

I was still working for George and was playing cards at a neighbouring farm one day when I started bragging about my motorbike and how I used to pull empty hay wagons with it. It was a beautiful wintery day with lots of snow. From the milk parlour where we were playing cards, I could see outside. I noticed a big pile of snow and figured it would be fun to drive through it with my bike. *No problem*, I thought. It would be a piece of cake and it would be fun. Because I didn't have my car, I asked someone to drive me to Ernie's place to fetch my bike. When we returned with it, I kicked the starter and to my utmost surprise it purred like a pussycat. I congratulated myself. I must have fixed it well.

By now I was being challenged to drive through that snow bank. It was about two metres high and three meters wide. I'd had a *few* drinks and I was feeling no pain, certainly no fear. I remember getting ready, judging the distance and taking the bike back about fifty metres…I kicked it into first gear, then second and then third. I was a flying superhero on wheels ready to plough through that *nothing* snow bank. However, fate did not dictate a victorious outcome for me! Within seconds I found myself sailing into the side of the adjacent barn head first without a helmet. I almost broke through the barn wall. I skinned both my knees and my mouth was full of snow and gravel. What I hadn't known was that there was a concrete water trough inside that innocent looking snow bank. It stopped my bike dead and sent me flying.

As for my precious three metre long 1942 Norton motorbike, well, it became a metre shorter. When I came out of my daze I was surprisingly coherent and in a fairly good mood. My friends were killing themselves laughing. I could have strangled them with my bare hands but I never blamed any of them. Could they have known there was a cement water trough in that snow bank? Did they know? I will never be certain. I did learn a good lesson though - before you dive into the water - or the snow - check the depth!

~

I survived that adventure until planting time, the following spring when a new hazard awaited me. I was working in a field when Mr. Markle Sr. called me over to his tractor to tell me something. The old man spoke with a British accent. His tractor had huge, two metre high tires. To hear him clearly and understand what he was saying I had to step in front of a tire. He was about seventy-five years old and probably not strong enough to keep the clutch pedal depressed for too long. For the life of me I couldn't make out what he was saying. This annoyed him because he fidgeted on his seat and let up on the clutch. The tractor lurched forward. I had but one second before I would have been run over. I hurtled my upper body out of the way and lived. Since I was not wearing a shirt there was an outline of soil on my chest replicating a tire track that could have been my executioner. The last time I moved that fast was when I was thirteen and found myself between two bumpers on railroad cars in my schoolyard.

~

Around the time this incident happened I got to know a very nice family; Frank and Ruby Berrisford and their two wonderful daughters Phyllis and Marion. My friend Hank Misters rented a room from the Berrisfords. I played a lot of Gin Rummy at their place, on a penny basis. I wonder - did I only go there for the entertaining game of cards?

Frank and I used to go to wrestling competitions at the Delta in Hamilton at least once a month. These marvellous matches were performed on a special deck in the middle of a swimming pool. When a wrestler became irritated by Al Bunny Dunlap, the referee, he'd throw Al into the water. Everyone would scream with delight. Frank loved wrestling even though he knew it was all fake. He used to be friends with "Killer Joe Christie" when he was simply known as Joe Kayorie of

Brantford. He went to Joe's funeral in 1999.

Frank and Ruby and I also used to often go dancing in Hamilton. Phyllis and Marion never came along so I had to look for honey in another hive. I remember driving down the Hamilton Mountain some Saturday evenings when it was so foggy that I had to sit on the hood of the car and verbally direct Frank to keep him on the road.

The Berrisfords were the two most wonderful people on earth and I enjoyed many good times with them. Frank lived to be eighty-seven and Ruby passed away at the age of ninety-two. Frank's mother was a lovely lady who lived to be over a hundred years old. She had a good sense of humour and loved to watch wrestling too. She reminded me of Queen Elizabeth. She was in great spirits until the day she died. I have often questioned why nice people can't live forever.

~

In 1960, I quit working for George Markle and secured a job with a construction company resurfacing highways in and around Brantford. Meanwhile George developed a water park on his farm which would have been successful had it not been for a terrible accident where someone drowned. I don't know the details but heard about the accident on the radio. After the park closed a consortium bought the entire property and developed a golf course. This course became known as the Heron Point Golf and Country Club. A few decades later I enjoyed playing on it and even visited the spot (which is now near a sand trap) where George's father almost ran me down with his tractor.

~

One of the resurfacing jobs I worked on was on Hwy 54 which went through Onondaga not far from that fire hall where we used to play cards. North of the village there was a little creek with a concrete bridge over it. That bridge had to be taken out and I got the pleasure of demolishing it with a jackhammer. All by myself. I finished the job in a week. My next job was a step up from the jackhammer - I was promoted to driving a water truck up and down the gravel road. The trick was to drive that truck down the road in reverse. After this job was completed, I was laid off.

Studying the English language relentlesly, was ongoing. I also began looking for another job. There had to be something closer to my actual trade - something that involved manufacturing and machinery.

Chapter Seventeen

I get a real job. ABEX turns out to be a good company. The manager appreciates my talents. Innovating is in my blood.

While browsing through a newspaper for jobs one day, I read a company named ABEX was hiring. I went there and applied for a job and was hired on the spot. The company manufactured tire molds. The molds were made of steel or aluminum, machined and cast. There were about five hundred people working there at that time.

I immediately got a good impression of the plant. It appeared the company was making some interesting products. Bill Handshumaker, a foreman in the finishing department, took me inside the shop and showed me the job he had in mind for me. His directions were straight forward and I understood everything he said. I liked him right off the bat. Later he turned out to be one of my favorite golfing partners, an awesome guy. He and his wife Milly lived not far from ABEX.

~

I started at 11 p.m. and was greeted by Bruce Greathead the night-shift lead hand in the finishing department. He gave me the tools I needed and showed me how to polish a tractor tire mold. He told me to come and see him if I had any questions. I didn't have any questions - in fact, I caught onto the job so well that I had the entire mold polished by 7 a.m. when the day shift started. It turned out the job was completed well ahead of schedule and more importantly it was properly done.

Bruce must have been checking my progress during the night and spoke to Bill in the morning because Bill came right over to me and inspected my work. Usually a polishing job like that took several shifts. Not only was it done quickly but the job looked really good, even to me. Of course Bill knew nothing about my artistic ability. To me, the mold wasn't any different from some work I had already done at school or the little tank I had polished and shown off with, on my graduation day. I still have that tank. I left it to my brother Attila in Hungary and he gave it back to me when I visited him at a later date.

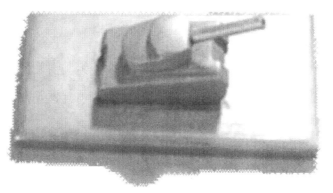

The little tank I made while at technical school.

As a result of having done such a good job, I was given the other half of the two-part mold to do. I also had the opportunity to match it to the one I had finished earlier. Matching molds means putting them together and blending the split line so that all the lugs and cavities were on the same plane, seamlessly.

For this procedure one had to put the two halves together and work on the inside of the mold, breathing in the abrasive dust. That part I didn't like very much because when I was in school I had learned about *silicosis,* a lung disease caused by dust from coal, cement and other materials. While I did the work I wore a felt mask, but had in mind to improve on the safety of that process when I had a chance. I wasn't about to rock the boat on my first days at work.

From there on I learned all the operations in the tire mold finishing business and within six months I became the lead hand in that department. Bruce was reassigned to another area. Bill the foreman, Joe Adams the superintendent, and Charley Daily the General Manager, were all happy to have gotten an employee who did his work so well.

~

Bill was a very charming fellow - funny, smart and a good golfer. He had a stocky build with a gentle face and a fair complexion. He always had a brush cut and he spoke with a pleasant southern accent and smoked good cigars. Bill appreciated the efforts and achievements of his workers and he gave people the opportunity to advance. He recognized those virtues in me and launched me onto my next *lily-pad* of life.

Milly his wife, was a trendy dresser. She was a brunette who liked to dress up even on week days. She too was from the south, a *Southern Belle.* In fact, she came from a family that was featured in *Life Magazine.* She was one of twenty-six children. Jay Hostatler, her brother also worked at ABEX as a tire mold finisher.

There was another remarkable chap in my shop, Ross Archer. He worked as a tire mold stamper.

The lettering on a rubber tire is raised whereas in a tire mold, it is recessed, stamped or engraved. Brand name, size of the tire, load and weight capacity etc. is usually stamped inside the mold.

Ross was a very personable guy and was liked by everyone. He had a lovely wife who came to all the company Christmas parties and picnics with him. He didn't know it yet, but cancer was ravaging his body.

Ross belonged to Jim's Gym on Pearl Street and walked past my apartment to get there. One Saturday he dropped in and we had a couple of beers and a long talk. He had been told about his disease and his story couldn't have made me any sadder. From then on he always came over to my place first and we went to work out together. I consoled him to the end. Ross first lost an arm to cancer and within three months he lost his life.

~

Wayne Gretzky and his father Walter also frequented Jim's Gym. I remember seeing Wayne doing pull-ups on a bar in the rear of the room. He was just a skinny little guy and didn't look to be very athletic at all. He looked like I had when I was eleven or twelve. Wayne wasn't famous yet in those days. I wonder if Wayne remembers me - I remember him!

~

Accidents can happen in any machine shop and ABEX was no exception.

One day a foreman named Joe decided to show a boring mill operator how to level a tire mold more quickly and efficiently. This particular mold was about one hundred and twenty centimetres in diameter and was fastened in with machine jaws. In order to get the mold levelled the machinist had to loosen the jaws slightly and hit the high side of the mold with a hammer made of lead. This would be done while the mold was turning slowly. With the lead hammer in his right hand and his eyes fixated on the indicator instrument, the machinist was ready to hit the tire mold when Joe stopped him. Joe placed his hand on an area of the mold and told the operator to hit the mold where his hand was. The machinist swung the lead hammer back, thinking Joe would surely move his hand away - but he didn't! A blood-curdling scream was heard throughout the shop. Everyone looked up in horror. Joe's hand was smashed so badly that he was off for several months. That was a bad accident.

~

Take Wayne's case for instance, an experienced milling machine operator who worked right in front of the engineering office. As I was going into the shop one day I noticed Wayne bending over a vice that had a steel object clamped into it. There was blood gushing from his head. With genuine concern I asked him what happened. He said he had hit his head with a hammer. That was of course, unbelievable to me. How could anyone hit themselves in the head with a hammer, I asked myself. I ran and got some paper towels and called an ambulance. I accompanied him to the hospital where he told me the whole story. In order to tighten the vice he would strike the lever with a hammer. Unfortunately this time, the lever sprung back and the hammer whacked him in the head. Wayne was off work for the rest of the week. Kind of reminds me of flying chuck keys.

Luckily no one in that factory ever died but scrapes and bruises did occur. Flexible grinder pulleys used to hang about head high. They had some guards but nevertheless, every so often someone would get their hair caught up in the pulley even though wearing a cap was policy.

Tire Molds

~

About a year after I started working for ABEX, I bought a classy little car - a black Karmann Ghia. I later customized it and painted it bright green.

One night, after dropping off my date I was stopped in the turning lane on the corner of West and Terrace Hill Streets ready to turn left. Through my rear view mirror, I watched in horror as a car approached at demonic speed. I couldn't do anything, I froze in my seat. My car was hit and was driven head-on into an oncoming Oldsmobile. I passed out instantly. My little car folded like an accordion. Thankfully the engine of my car was in the rear or I would have been crushed to death.

When I came to, I found all my lower teeth had been loosened. I had suffered a concussion and I had bruises all over my body. I think the tow truck driver either drove me home or took me to the hospital. I don't remember. The guy that hit me from behind was a lawyer and he hired one of his "buddies" to represent him in court. He was in the wrong and he was drunk. He got off with a slap on the wrist. I got a few bucks out of that crash but I'd sooner have had my beautiful customized Karmann Ghia back.

With the extra money I bought a new Pontiac Strato- Chief. This car was a boat compared to my Karmann Ghia.

Top, left – a self-portrait;
Charles and his cars; his friend Marion; uncle Alex in
the USA; in the snow outside his apartment.

Chapter Eighteen

My uncle Alex should have been an opera singer and my cousin Alex Jr. a Toreador.

As you might have guessed by now, I didn't make it to the United States. Uncle Alex never sent me the new immigration papers and I didn't persist. I had become quite settled in Canada. However, uncle Alex did start coming to see me two or three times a year. He usually visited with his brother-in-law Johnny – 'Johnny Bull' my uncle usually called him. Johnny was a third generation Mohawk and he used to be a baker. He was a skinny guy. He was funny and always had a joke or three to tell. His daughter Betty was married to Alex Jr. and she was an eternal blonde, very easy on the eyes.

Uncle Alex was a big fellow with red hair. He had a very responsible job at Firestone in Akron, Ohio. He supervised a rubber extrusion machine. He held that position for forty years. He drove Buicks all his life and bought a new one every three years. And boy, could he sing. He knew a lot of old Hungarian songs and ballads even I hadn't heard of. When he started singing everyone's jaw dropped open. He could have been an opera singer for sure and I think there still are some people who can attest to that.

In his later years his sister Mary did his cooking but he always loved my cabbage rolls and stuffed peppers the best. Whenever I went to visit him I made his favorite – cabbage rolls.

~

The Yambor family and Johnny's family lived in Akron not too far from each other.

Alex Jr. used to be a travelling salesman for a company and for his outstanding performance he was awarded a trip to Mexico.

During his Mexican vacation while at a bull fighting arena, he volunteered to fight a baby bull and it upended him. He was taken out on a stretcher. Everyone clapped thinking it was staged. The next day he couldn't move. After spending a few months in and out the hospital, he had to quit travelling and find a sedentary job. Sometimes he had three jobs. I have to hand it to him he was a very responsible guy. He raised four kids; Diana, Rocky, Jackie and Joey and provided a good living for Betty.

~

Willy, my sister and Alex Jr.

One particular summer weekend Alex Jr., Betty, Rocky, Diana, Willy and Irene came to visit. Boy, did we have fun! We packed a lot of activity into that weekend and did a lot of joking around. I took Diana and Rocky down to the Port Dover beach in my convertible to show then off but mainly to show off Diana 'the blond bombshell'. Later Willy and Alex Jr. accompanied me to the beer store. I had to stand in line because it was very busy. The two of them were hanging around waiting for me. Suddenly someone tapped me on the shoulder. As I turned around Alex Jr. grabbed me by my waist and kissed me on the lips. I damn near fainted from embarrassment. The whole place was howling and Alex and Willy were rolling on the floor laughing. Whenever I go to that beer store the two regular employees Mike and Bill, always ask me; "Where's your boyfriend?" Both of these dear relatives passed away in 2012—Alex Jr. was eighty-two and Willy was eighty-five. *Hasta La Vista* dear brothers, we sure had fun.

~

Around the mid 1980's Willy's son, Billy Kovacs, had a terrible accident. Billy was a linesman who almost lost his life while on the job. He was high up on a hydro pole when his back came in contact with a live ten thousand volt wire. It shorted out through a drill that he was holding pressed to his stomach. When he was brought down off the pole his mouth had to be pried open with a screwdriver so he could be resuscitated. He had dozens of skin grafts both on his back and stomach and suffered severe pain for a long time. Thankfully he lived and is now doing relatively well. My incident with the light bulb at Mr. Pup's shop was nothing in comparison to this.

Karen, his sister had been killed in a car accident around the same time. The Kovacs family sure had its share of disasters that year. Today, Billy comes to visit with his wife Linda and occasionally they bring Billy's son Clayton and his wife Jesse. Jesse makes delicious pumpkin cookies. I love them and my cholesterol loves them too. Both Billy and Linda are retired and they bought a hobby farm where Linda raises Long Horn cattle – you ought to see them – they're amazing! While Linda manages the cattle, Billy enjoys deer hunting on his farm.

Chapter Nineteen

My hemorrhoid treatment beats medieval torture. I start painting abstracts.

Before I get too far ahead of myself, I want to go back to ABEX where my 'ascent to the top' happened very rapidly. I must have been a *shooting star* - there just wasn't enough of me to go around. In the span of about two years I went from mold finisher, to lead hand, to inspector, to foreman in the EDM (Electrical Discharge Machine) department. This last position transfer took place when the regular EDM foreman fainted in the middle of the shop. An event that could have been caused by the incredible pressure these foremen were under day after day. I took his position temporarily, to manage the department. Since I knew relatively little about that job, I had no pressure at all.

Incidentally, at the same time as my temporarily changing jobs, one of the machine operators, George Harris, won first prize in an English lottery and we never saw him again. He just disappeared. I think the prize was three hundred thousand dollars - equal to about $2.2 million today.

It took a few months, but the company found an appropriate replacement for the EDM department and I continued being quality inspector.

During this time I also developed a bad case of haemorrhoids. So bad that I figured I would need an operation. Charley Daily the General Manager, who had become a good friend, just happened to be in the shop, so I called him over and told him I'd be off for a few days because I needed to have haemorrhoid surgery. I told him I'd be back as soon as I could. He knew I was a hard worker and wouldn't miss a day if I didn't have a good reason. Then, he asked me to come into his office.

He told me I should go and see this particular doctor in Toronto who was using a new method of treating haemorrhoids. This new procedure wouldn't require me to have an operation. He said it would only take a few hours and I would be back to work quickly. Charley even made the phone call and set up an appointment for me. I was happy as a lark that I didn't need an operation after all!

However, after what happened at that private clinic; I remember thinking that I wished I had gone ahead with the surgery. I will always refer to this clinic as a torture chamber. The doctor used a pincher-like device to secure a rubber band around one of the haemorrhoids. At that instant I thought I was going to rocket through the roof. Never in my life had I experienced pain even close to that. Well, maybe once - back in Hungary, when a dentist ground away relentlessly on a bad tooth without any anesthetic, in an effort to try to fit me with a bridge.

The moment this cruel man secured another rubber 'O' ring to the second haemorrhoid, I inhaled deeply, and instantly perspiration began cascading down my body – like Niagara Falls. The pain was unbearable. When the procedure was over he immediately handed me a pill and gave me more to take later. I think he must have given me pure cocaine or some other potent narcotic. The pain stopped and I felt like I was in *la-la land.* I managed to drive and I had no more pain until I got home, a good hour later. Then the pain started up again. I took the next pill, but this second pill did not give me much relief at all.

At that time, I lived in an apartment with a friend, Zoli Toth. He watched me walk around the kitchen island in excruciating pain for hours on end. He felt sorry for me. To make matters worse, with the pain only slightly dimmed, I had to go to work the next morning. I was extremely disillusioned. Incredibly I had four more sessions with that masochistic maniac, each time dying a thousand deaths. In the end, after almost a year of torture, I had to have surgery anyway.

~

I don't think a haemorrhoid operation is a big deal and as with any surgery, there is a procedure that has to be adhered to. Just before the operation they put me to sleep. When I came to I was totally paralysed and desperately wanted to move my toes. When I couldn't, I screamed for the nurse to come and help me. Once my toes wiggled I was okay. I didn't know why she was laughing. Was I the only one to ever have had frozen toes like that? The operation was totally painless. In

fact, I drove myself home from the hospital the same afternoon. This event occurred in the summertime. I remember because I suntanned on a blanket in front of my apartment after getting home. I took care to follow post surgery instructions and the surgery was a total success and I was cured. I felt like a brand new man.

In order to fill my spare time, I started painting. I had experience working with watercolours but wanted a change. I wanted to try a new medium - plastic paint.

I made some unusual painting tools and knives and finished about a dozen paintings of different sizes and on diverse surfaces. I thought my paintings were imaginative and my style unique. I generated some admirers but, none with money. My acquaintances were everyday normal people.

Persistently, I kept taking my artwork to exhibitions at places like the Glenhyrst Art Gallery of Brantford. Some people thought my abstract art was cool. Personally, I really like my paintings. They have imagination and class. Especially, the ones I named: *How the West Was Won; Colt 45; and July 1st Celebration.* I didn't sell any of my abstracts. I did give some away. Maybe the longer I keep these paintings hidden the more they will be worth. Maybe they'll sell for millions after I kick the bucket!

In the meantime I started to write poetry, short stories, and music.

Chapter Twenty

*I befriend a B.F. Goodrich inspector. My friends
are also talented in many ways.*

We did a lot of good work at ABEX and we also had a great deal of fun. We used to play the card game Twenty-One, during the midnight shift and we could hardly wait to finish that shift so we could go to Lou Seaman's house to continue our game.

Lou was one of our favourite colleagues. He was an old-fashioned Hungarian man with a pleasant accent and he was a sausage-maker! When we got to his house he would break out the food and we would eat like horses. He loved to show off with his home-smoked bacon, ham, sausages and venison. He also smoked trout, salmon, and pickerel. Every fall, he and his hunting buddies went up north, and they always came back from their trip with at least a couple of deer or moose. We couldn't stop praising him, and he just loved to be complimented.

Lou also made wine and moonshine, and if we didn't watch ourselves, we could get pickled pretty quickly. Some fellows did, and ended up losing their money. Sometimes we were up for three days playing Twenty-One. In the end I think Lou came out ahead of the game. But then his wife left him. She no doubt got tired of the cigarette smoke, the constant noise in the house and mountains of dishes to wash every day. They got back together twenty years later, but Lou died shortly afterwards.

~

ABEX did a lot of work for US tire manufacturers, and their inspectors used to arrive from various companies and often stayed for days. After I became head of quality control, Charley Daily gave me the *back-breaking* job of entertaining these inspectors after hours, by taking them out to dinner at restaurants in and around Brantford. "Accommodate them," Charley would say. "The happier the inspectors are, the more work we'll get."

One of my favourite restaurants was the John Peel, a fine dining place similar to the Barbarian Steak House on Elm Street, in Toronto. I don't think there are many places that served a better Greek salad or prime rib like the John Peel used to.

There is one young inspector in particular that I'll never forget - Dennis Pakren. He worked for B.F. Goodrich and he could hardly wait to get out of the shop and head out for the evening. He did his job diligently but he was always happiest when he knew I too had inspected the mold. Tire molds had to be flawless.

Dennis enjoyed good food and craved entertainment. As instructed, I showed him a good time. We went to many restaurants. At the Erie Beach Hotel in Port Dover, for example, Dennis would order a two-inch steak - blue. After he finished it he would order another one exactly the same. I couldn't even watch him eat. He loved to go to places like Starvin Marvin in Toronto or the Barbarian Steak House. I only had one problem entertaining these inspectors; I was gaining weight from all the rich food.

Whenever an inspector wanted to go golfing, my best friend Andy Gunn would occasionally help out. He was a machine shop foreman and unlike myself, he was a seasoned golfer. Most of the time though he was even busier than I was, and needed to be on the job. I had no choice: I had to train others to inspect the tire molds and

I had to get good at playing golf! As time went by my game improved and I became a pretty good golfer. I had a 'hole-in-one' three times which is more than many golfers have ever had.

Our shop had a golf league and almost everyone belonged to it. Just to name a few - Charley Daily, manager; Bill Handshumaker, finish line foreman; Bruce Greathead, lead hand; Joe Adams, superintendent; Art Belair, machine shop foreman; Dennis Materic, scheduling; Andy Gunn, engraving machines; Bob Rutherford, lead hand and many others.

When I transferred to the engineering department, I looked after all the golf-related business. Each week I posted the scores on a communal sheet where everyone could see their progress. Some players, whose names I mentioned above were notorious winners. On field days however, since everyone had a handicap, the first prize was up for grabs to anyone. Generally speaking though, the winner was the person who had the least to drink.

We had fabulous prizes and everyone got one. We usually stayed for dinner at the golf club and afterwards buses would drive us back to the plant. There's no need to talk about the bus trips to and from the golf course; all that needs to be said is that there was booze - both ways.

Our home golf course was either Northridge or Lynn Meadows where the competition was fierce. One year I wrote a hole by hole parody of a game - showcasing Art Belair and myself and it was hilarious. I still have copy of that satire, which today I would call somewhat simplistic, but true.

The company golf league ended at ABEX when many of us left for JAX but we continued a league with the new company as well. I still looked after the scoreboard but things weren't the same. I missed the old crew - the camaraderie, the competition and the good old boys. JAX seemed more like a rat race.

The ABEX crew, Charley Daily standing in front, I took the picture.

Golf became a large and important part of my life. While living with Zoli Toth, we played hundreds of games together at the Arrowdale and Northridge Golf courses in Brantford. Many times on the weekend we would play four rounds per day - rain or shine – and would eat hamburgers on the run.

This blows my mind: When it would start raining and thundering people would get off the golf course or stand under trees. Not Zoli or I! We would take the opportunity to play through. Hole after hole we would either par or birdie - in the rain and we didn't get hit by lightning! Today though, we would never play in a rainstorm - that's just insane. We know better now. I was a five handicapper in those days. (matching my IQ)?

~

I remember going to the World's Fair in New York with Zoli, in 1964. We stayed in a hotel on Broadway and went to see an 'Ed Sullivan' show. On the way there I got a ticket for going six miles over the speed limit. I think the ticket was for thirty-four dollars. The cops were concealed around a bend and were stopping everyone. It was strange because they didn't take cash which they usually do, but instead they sent me a ticket in the mail. I paid it. I thought about this and figured out that taking the cash would only have slowed them down.

Zoli was a little guy, one hundred and sixty centimetres tall and he ate like a horse and drank like a fish. He and his buddy Ted used to perform in public schools doing gymnastics like professional acrobats. Their inspirational efforts and perseverance in the community should have been recognized in some way but that never happened.

Zoli on top, me on the right.

I clearly remember Zoli and I visiting Niagara Falls. He was doing handstands on the railing. People stopped to admire him. They thought he was a performer, a stunt man. If I'd had a hat, I could have collected money.

~

In the summer Zoli and Ted and a few other high energy guys like me used to put on a show at the Waterford ponds. After Zoli got married, he settled down. He outgrew the stunting except when he and I got together. We did some acrobatic stunts like jumping from the floor up onto the kitchen counter. You had to keep your feet together and jump straight up. I made it every time but Zoli, being shorter, missed a few times and bruised his legs on the edge of the counter top.

While he was no gymnast Mike Szilagyi, Zoli's friend was an extremely good card player and a fun guy to hang out with. Zoli introduced Mike to me and he became my friend too. Mike was from the same village in Hungary as Zoli and they had known each other since grade school albeit neither knew they had both landed in Brantford. They ran into each other, quite by accident at the Brantford Hungarian Hall.

Mike married Mary and they started a family together. They had two daughters; Susan and Rose and a son Denis. They now have several grandchildren. Mike retired from Budd's in Kitchener and Mary from Dare's. Today Mike and Mary do a great deal of community work. For decades they were involved with the Kitchener Kossuth Club and its early development. They are hardworking responsible people - the kind that helped to build Canada. Their name made it into my first book; *Tusks of Terror*.

Zoli and his wife Marg were equally as industrious and hardworking. They raised two daughters Anita and Laura. Zoli has two grandchildren. Our dear friend Marg has passed on but I'm sure she's in a happier place,

I had another buddy Zolly Szabo. I taught him how to golf. He eventually became a better golfer than I. His wife Gail is a remarkably good golfer too. I was surprised to see her drive just like a professional. They have one son Steven who is an industrial engineer and is married to Latha and they have a son, Ethan. Ethan is talented and good at sports like hockey and lacrosse.

Even though I was busy with several hobbies, with my job and my inventions, Zolly and I shared some good times in Myrtle Beach, South Carolina. We played most of the golf courses there. Zolly was skilled at tennis, ping pong and pool and probably many other things that I didn't even know about. However when it came to chess, we were equal.

Zolly never returned to Hungary for a visit because he thought the Russians would arrest him the minute he stepped off the plane. In 1956, while making an escape from Hungary, he was caught at the Austrian border and was locked up in a makeshift jail. He picked the lock, nabbed a machine pistol and shot his way out. He escaped into the countryside and found refuge in a barn, hiding himself in a stack of hay. The soldiers that were looking for him were stabbing into the haystacks indiscriminately and one of them drove a bayonet through his left bicep. He crunched his teeth and remained quiet. He made it across the border the next night where he was treated in a hospital. Zolly too is gone now. He passed away August 27, 2009.

~

I don't know how I found the time to go golfing, hang out at the German Club, go dancing every Saturday and socialize. I was living the life of a minor celebrity. Anyone that played soccer for the German Club was automatically considered a celebrity. We, namely the single guys, had groupies - not like the Rolling Stones and the Beatles but close.

I started playing soccer for the German Club in 1962 and always played right-centre because I was quick. I was no soccer star though - none of us were. I don't think we ever won anything of any great importance but we had a good time.

Chapter Twenty-one

I befriend a real lumberjack – Fred. He disappears then reappears. I invent my Trace-A-Toon's. I get married! We go to Europe.

I was a member of the German Canadian Club in Brantford where I spent most Saturday evenings either dancing or working behind the bar when my turn came up. This club was started on the upper floor of a building on King Street in downtown Brantford. The steps to the club led straight up from the street as if they were leading to heaven; or for some others from upstairs they were leading straight down to hell. Since I played soccer for the club I spent considerable time at the bar.

From time to time the place would get chaotic. A lot of things can happen in a dance hall or in a bar. In order to save the club from complete destruction and perhaps serious injury to patrons, they hired a bouncer. His name was Fred and he was a big German fellow who used to be a lumberjack. I've seen wine barrels smaller in diameter than Fred's chest. I am a friendly sort of a guy and semi-smart, so I thought if I bought Fred some drinks he'd like me and go easy on me when or if, I got myself into any unexpected or uncontrollable *tight* situations.

After Fred's arrival on the scene things were peaceful and proper for a stretch of time - maybe three days. One Saturday evening there was a disturbance on the dance floor. Not with me, because I was working behind the bar, but with a person I knew - a fellow Hungarian. He was a tough guy - tougher than me - but not as tough as Fred.

Noticing the disturbance, Fred walked onto the

dance floor and at that moment you could hear a pin drop. Fred grabbed the troublemaker by the seat of his pants and by the scruff of his collar and marched him out into the hall. From there he heaved the fellow down those stairs. He tumbled head over heels all the way down. I gasped and thought the man was dead for sure! I looked at Fred, and he appeared totally calm. Nonchalantly he dusted off his palms. Someone hurried down the stairs to check on the guy. He was okay. We figured he had to have been quite drunk and relaxed because he wasn't hurt.

I remained friends with Fred for a long time and felt incredibly safe when he was around. Fred was married to a German lady, Alma, but when their

Erika and Charles on their wedding day.

marriage fell apart he moved back to Germany. This is not the end of this story, rather the beginning.

~

I met my wife Erika at the German Club. 'I saw her standing there' - just like in that Beatles song - and the rest was easy. She worked in the kitchen at St. Joseph's hospital and I was making good money at a solid job. We courted for several months before I proposed and she accepted. We were married on April 8, 1967 and Zolly Szabo was my best man. We moved into the same apartment where Zoli

Toth and I had lived.

~

We planned our honeymoon in August, and went on a trip to Germany. We landed in Frankfurt and spent the first night with Erika's family.

When we awoke in the morning I heard a voice that I thought I recognized even though it was spoken in German. Erika said it was impossible that I should recognize a voice on the other side of the ocean. I had to agree with her, I had to be mistaken.

However, upon walking from the bedroom, to my greatest astonishment I saw Fred, the Brantford German Club bouncer, standing in the kitchen! It turned out that he was Erika's uncle through his marriage to Alma. Alma's brother Rudy was Erika's father - small world. We kissed and hugged and if I remember correctly I even punched him in his beer gut - not hard though - just for fun. Thankfully he didn't punch me back.

After his divorce, Fred married a German lady. Fred is deceased now. Alma also remarried and is still living in Alberta. Fred's second wife is also still living happily in Germany - without him. I had heard rumours that Fred was hard on his women. Fred truly exerted himself during our stay in Germany. He drove us everywhere and did whatever he could for us.

Unfortunately fate was not kind to Erika and I on our honeymoon. We left Germany later that week, rented a car and drove to Budapest. My family was elated when we arrived. It was only the second time I had returned to Hungary after leaving for Canada. My brother was now twenty-three and my sister was eleven. The unimaginable happened—Erika became ill and had to be hospitalized with a burst appendix. After that - *total chaos* would be the best way to describe our vacation. She spent the rest of our honeymoon in a hospital and I damn near went crazy. She nearly lost her life. It was an unbelievable event for both of us. The doctors in Budapest saved her.

When it was time to fly back to Canada she wasn't well enough to travel and I had to sign her out of the hospital. Erika was very happy to be home and gradually recovered.

~

While I was staying with my family I noticed my little sister playing with some plastic animal silhouettes. She was projecting them onto walls using a flashlight and making them dance. An idea occurred to me... what if I created an assortment of silhouettes with Disney characters? I figured Donald Duck, Pluto, Goofy and some others would make a splendid collection. I did some research and in 1968 obtained a license from Disney and designed a mold for six Disney characters I eventually called '*Trace-A-Toons*'.

Around the same time Charley Daily announced his retirement from ABEX. Since we had become good friends, he wanted to be my partner to look after marketing *Trace-A-Toons*. I would handle the manufacturing part of the business. Things were beginning to fall nicely into place. However Jack Thornton, the sales manager at ABEX also announced his departure from ABEX at that time and he wanted to hire me as his engineering manager for his new company. In fact he needed me to start immediately on the blue prints for a new plant -'JAX Mold and Machine Ltd.' on Donly Drive in Simcoe, Ontario.

Despite this new job development I carried on with my Disney characters. Clem Saila, a Disney representative under Creative Designs Co. in Toronto was handling all my business with Disney.

Charley and I set out to conquer the world and went to a toy show at Place Bonaventure in Montreal.

We were doing really well. However fate was against me again. Like lightning from a clear blue sky Charley announced he had cancer and had to quit immediately. I nearly lost my mind. What could I do? I had to make up my mind in a hurry.

Busy with company drawings, entertaining customers, manufacturing my *Trace-A-Toon* characters and having to handle marketing as well, left me totally overwhelmed. Something had to give. I couldn't find another person to partner with and since my bread and butter came from JAX, I had to sacrifice my Disney project - a decision I regret to this day.

I still have the original drawings of Disney's Donald Duck, Pluto, Mickey, Winnie the Pooh, King Louie and Baloo and some others as well. The idea is not dead. I have even innovated on the concept further.

WALT DISNEY PRODUCTIONS
character merchandising division
477 MADISON AVENUE · NEW YORK, N.Y. 10022

April 21, 1969

Charles E. Jambor Company
c/o Ballachey, Moore & Hart
P. O. Box 1022, 88 Nelson Street
Brantford, Ontario, Canada

Gentlemen:

In compliance with your request for an extension of your contract with us, dated
January 19, 1968 , which contract (including amendments thereto, if any)
is herein referred to as the "basic contract", we hereby mutually agree that the
said basic contract be and the same is hereby extended for an additional period
of   one (1) year   commencing on   April 1, 1969
and terminating on March 31, 1970.

This extension is made in consideration of:

> Two Hundred and Fifty ($250.00) Dollars, payable upon the signing
> of this agreement, receipt of which we hereby acknowledge.

Said sum is an advance on account of royalties to accrue during the extended
period covered hereby, and the amount of said advance shall be deductible from
the amount of royalties (if any) accruing during the said extended period. If
the amount of said royalties shall, however, be insufficient to cover the said
advance, neither said advance nor any portion thereof shall be repayable to you.

This extension shall be governed in accordance with the terms, conditions and pro-
visions of the said basic contract, and by affixing your signature under the word
"accepted" provided below, you will be deemed to have reaffirmed the terms of
said contract and to have agreed to the renewal hereinabove set forth.

Very truly yours,

WALT DISNEY PRODUCTIONS

ACCEPTED:

CHARLES E. JAMBOR COMPANY   By _____

By _____
   (Title)   Proprietor

NO AGREEMENT WILL BE BINDING ON THIS CORPORATION UNLESS IN WRITING AND SIGNED BY AN OFFICER

Chapter Twenty-two

There is a scream in the night. We buy our first house. We have two daughters born on the same day – two years apart. We go to Europe again.

For the first few months at JAX Mold and Machine Ltd., Andy Gunn and I travelled from Brantford to Simcoe every day until we both found a place to live in Simcoe. Andy bought a house opposite the Simcoe Mall on Hwy 3 and I bought one on Union Street. Both houses were old. Andy's was much bigger which definitely came in handy for the seven kids he and his wife Shirley had.

~

I was a busy man! By day I was JAX plant engineer and by night I was making drawings for the new plant on Donly Drive. I also worked on a new tire mold engraving machine in the evenings. Andy became the plant superintendent and this new tire mold shop was producing molds by the third week of operation. I kept a steel chip from the very first mold ever made. Once we moved from the temporary location into the new building, life continued much the same way as it had at ABEX. The only difference was that I had a lot more drawing and design work to do and the pace of activities was ratcheted up by about five hundred percent.

~

Andy had a swimming pool at his house and I was in it at least once a week over the summer. I loved his kids and wished I had some of my own. Rick was Andy's oldest followed by Jamie, Marilee and Andrea. Shirley's kids were Tina, Mike, and Wendy.

167

One day Andy came into his kitchen looking as though he'd had a fight with a bear. He was telling us he'd rolled his lawn mower over on a grade by his house. I wasn't too happy hearing that, and he admitted he should have known better. Had the machine rolled over him he could have been killed. I don't know where he bought it from, but that old lawn mower resembled a regular tractor. I never liked that machine—it just didn't look right to me. It looked disproportionate. The seat was way up high about a metre off the ground. After that accident, he fixed the steering wheel and a few bent parts, but eventually got rid of it.

~

That same summer we re-grouted Andy's pool and painted it blue. We painted the Canadian flag onto the middle of the pool floor. When we were finished we had a big party with several colleagues from the shop attending.

Andy had a sour cherry tree orchard in his backyard and I remember making about thirty bottles of cherry wine from those pickings. I put the bottles in my fruit cellar and forgot about them. When I rearranged the shelves thirty years later I found the bottles and was overjoyed. The wine turned out to be really good. I still have some of it preserved.

~

Canada's Prime Minister, Pierre Elliott Trudeau and his wife Margaret, had been blessed with two sons born on the same day two years apart. Erika and I would not be outdone. Our first daughter Barbara Elaine (Bobbi) was born on April 24, 1972 and two years later on the same date we welcomed our second daughter, Carol Ann (Carrie). Erika had healthy pregnancies and although both births were by C-section, everyone was just fine. Both of our daughters have grown into smart and beautiful women but I'll let them tell their own stories when they write their own autobiographies. We have four wonderful grandchildren - Lia, Lucas and Erik and Kage. They are all on the right track.

~

Willy and Irene came to visit us from Akron, Ohio. After a busy day we were happy to go to bed. In this old house on Union St. we only had one finished bedroom and it was downstairs. The upstairs rooms weren't yet done. Erika and I slept on a pull-out sofa as we offered Willy and Irene our bed. It was a hot summer night and we had no air conditioning. Willy got up in the middle of the night to open a window which seemed a simple enough task. However it proved to be anything but.

The window was of the old fashioned type that would be held in place by a counter-weight in the frame when opened. Since our house was at least a hundred years old the counterweight might have been broken or lost and simple friction would not have been sufficient to keep the window up. Willy pushed the window open and expected it to stay there but it didn't. It crashed down on his hands. Had the window remained open, his desperate scream in the night would have woken up the whole town. But the window wasn't open; it was closed and resting on his crunched knuckles.

After I recovered from my laughing fit I asked him "Why did you leave your hands on the window sill?" He couldn't answer me because he was in too much pain.

~

Dennis Pakren the tire mold inspector from B.F. Goodrich, resurfaced and I had to accommodate him again. By this time Erika and I had moved into our new home on Oak Street and our Bobbi was about eight months old. I didn't feel like driving Dennis around like I used to, I just wanted to stay close to Simcoe. I asked him if he would rather play ping pong on my table downstairs than drive around to bars. Big mistake! He loved ping pong - we ended up playing all night! I never played that game again!

After spending the night playing ping pong, Dennis went to his motel took a quick shower and was back at the shop inspecting molds until three o'clock that afternoon. He still had the energy to go out to hotels that night! Luckily I had enough energy myself to keep up with him. I had to watch my drinking though because I did all the driving and I needed a clear head for my design work as well.

At one point, Dennis told me he was quitting his job. He had purchased a bar in Lodi, Ohio. He could hardly wait to have me visit there. I was elated. No more late nights, eating rich food and no more driving to Toronto! Boy, was I wrong. Other inspectors came from other tire companies with similar demands. Some liked fine food, some liked golf, some liked bars.

My work kept piling up, I was overwhelmed again. I had to hire a draughtsman to help with my drawings but the design work I still did myself. I was a major contributor to a so-called *mechanical tire mold.* At about this time, I re-designed the lettering of the 'B.F. Goodrich' logo. This lettering was also used on other brand name tire products for cars and trucks. Today, they still use the same *Helvetica* lettering that I had used.

~

I went to B.F. Goodrich in Akron quite often, and on one of those occasions I stopped for a visit at Willy's place. After I told him about Dennis and his bar in Lodi (which is practically in his backyard) he looked forward to seeing Dennis and his bar. Willy used to drive for a beer company in Lodi and was surprised he had never heard of Dennis or his bar. As it turned out, that particular place was just outside of Willy's territory.

The day we went there, a biker gang was also there and when they found out I was from Canada, they all wanted to buy us drinks. Since Willy already a couple of beer and was doing the driving, we only had one drink and left. Dennis had dancers in the evenings and he wanted us to stay. We didn't.

Shorty after Dennis got married, his wife didn't want competition so, she made him sell the bar and Dennis started another new chapter in his life.

~

In 1974 JAX sent me to Europe, specifically Germany, to design some essential equipment for an Italian tire manufacturing company, Pirelli. The plant was near Nuremberg close to Karlsruhe where Erika was born. We decided we should take the opportunity and make this excursion a family holiday, and booked a three-week trip. We drove on the Autobahn which is an experience in and of itself. Along the Autobahn, all the rest stops had a 'Welcome Centre' and they were all out of this world. It was a pleasure to change or even bathe a baby or older child there. These rooms were always bright and spotless and well equipped with diapers, towels, soap and more items than you could possibly think of. They had coffee, milk, snacks and fruit available too. This service was attached to the restaurant, was free, and even had maps to other family room locations displayed as well as emergency numbers. They were truly amazing.

~

Speed is nothing unusual on the Autobahn. The highway is as smooth as pool table top. We saw motorbikes going two hundred and fifty kilometres an hour and Lamborghinis doing three hundred. We knew this because we were driving a rented Fiat that had a top speed of two hundred kilometres and these other cars and bikes were flying past us as if we were stopped. The posted speed limit is two hundred kilometres an hour.

The food in Germany was good but we found that all the restaurants served their meat with a sauce on top. I specifically asked the waiter for no sauce on my steak and he still brought it with sauce. I guess he couldn't imagine it otherwise. I sent it back and ordered a hamburger. Even that came with a sauce!

After visiting Erika's relatives we drove on to Austria and then on to Hungary.

When we arrived in Vienna, we drove around the inner city turnabout at least eight times before figuring out which exit to take to M1, the main highway to Budapest. If there is any significance to traffic turnabouts it is this: it's a great way to make sure your ads get seen! There were at least ten thousand signs and nine thousand nine hundred and ninety of them were advertisements leaving very few actual directional route signs.

~

Being in Budapest for the second time was exciting for Erika. The city amazed her and she enjoyed exploring it. She had a car! The only people that drove cars in communist Budapest in those days were foreigners. That explained the attention she got whenever she parked the car and got out. The vehicle had Austrian license plates. One time she stopped beside a truck full of Russian soldiers who were almost falling out of their vehicle watching her every move. Their reaction made her very uncomfortable as she thought they were going to interrogate her.

In those days, when shopping in stores, customers were not allowed to touch and examine packaged garments let alone try them on! Those were the days when sales clerks were allowed to beat customers up for unwrapping packages. Imagine that.

Erika found shopping in Budapest quit peculiar and did mostly window shopping. She did buy some unique things.

~

My dad didn't have room for all of us.
Because Erika and I and the babies were going to be around for several weeks, my dad had arranged a place for us to stay. Mrs. Pup, a neighbour was more than delighted to take us in. Mr. Pup had passed on by then. We slept there and she could hardly wait to cook for us. She insisted on looking after our two little girls giving us a chance to visit old acquaintances and tour around the city. We paid Mrs. Pup well for her hospitality and greatly enjoyed our time in her home.

~

Our trip provided a good opportunity for catching up with family. My dad and I, Attila my brother and Aniko my sister talked a lot and I did a lot of singing with some old friends. On several occasions we went out to dine at places that I was never able to afford in my younger days. I was happy to be able to treat my family.

Attila had become a machinist and he appreciated the digital Vernier callipers and the carbide tool tips that I brought for him. He worked in his little shop in his garage. Often times he partnered with Joe Vinklar on larger projects.

Joe and his wife Eta along with Joe's Canadian uncle had surprised me with a visit once, here in Canada. I almost fainted when I saw him at my front door. I remember it was a rainy day and Erika was at work. I turned the TV on for them while I ran out for some Kentucky Fried Chicken. We had some good laughs and talked about the many experiences we had shared. I promised I'd come and see him at his home the next time I visited Hungary – which I obviously did.

Joe had purchased a cottage near Lake Balaton and we stayed there for a few days and had a great time. It was a nice place and I remember seeing a mounted *fogas* on the cottage wall. This is a type of European fish with lots of teeth and is full of bones and not good to eat.

I called Joe on his birthday every February 8 and we would have a good talk - and cry.

~

During our visit to Budapest we noticed Russian soldiers were everywhere. They were friendly enough but were also jealous of Hungary's advanced living standards. The lucky ones who found a Hungarian wife were allowed to stay in Hungary.

Chapter Twenty-three

I lose a hundred dollar US bill - and find it. We travel over two hundred kilometres per hour yet our luggage passes us.

When we left Hungary, we took our time driving back to the Frankfurt airport. On an evening after arriving in Austria, we went to the same little chalet we had stayed in at the beginning of our journey. We got there around eleven in the evening and the place was full. The owners were very nice and helped us with finding a place to stay in the next village. We were in luck – there was a room available for us. To get to this hotel, we drove on the most winding road I've ever seen in my life. We had to pay in advance, which was no surprise. I reached in my wallet and to my greatest shock I found it was empty. "Holy mackerel"! I said (not my exact wording). I thought for a moment and remembered I had already had the money in my hand back at the chalet. I told Erika I had to return there. I was sweating blood. I drove like crazy back down that treacherous road.

As soon as I got out of my car, I saw the money. It was a miracle. The folded one hundred dollar bill was lying right in the middle of the sidewalk under a street lamp, no less. I dove for it and just in the nick of time too. A man walking along was a mere few steps away from that hundred dollar bill. That was pure and sheer luck. In the morning, we continued on to Frankfurt.

~

Driving on the Autobahn again, I found my self gathering momentum going down a hill and exceeding the two hundred kilometres an hour posted speed limit so I eased on the brake. As I did this I saw something familiar out of the corner of my eye. It was our luggage passing us! Erika was shouting for me to stop. She had heard a click that sounded like straps breaking or something coming undone on the car roof luggage carrier. In total befuddlement I pulled over to the shoulder of the road and got out. The two suitcases were sitting in the middle of the Autobahn! Cars were flying by like bullets. In a momentary lull I jumped out to grab the suitcases but was only able to retrieve one. The other one had to wait a few more minutes for another break in the traffic. I could see the securing strap had snapped. I stacked them onto the back seat of the car and our poor girls were really crammed together. Thankfully we didn't have too much further to go. Amazingly, when we unpacked the bags at home, several bottles and ceramic artifacts were completely intact.

~

We arrived at the airport early in the afternoon. Using our Visa card we checked into Holiday Inn for the night. It was a Sunday and the stores were closed. We couldn't buy beer anywhere not even in the hotel. Someone suggested that we try a downtown convenience store that sold beer in a six-pack. I bought a case and brought it back to the hotel. When I opened a bottle and tasted it, I almost threw up. I have never in my life tasted anything so vile. It was a brown beer and was supposed to be good for you. It was good for me all right - it cured me of ever wanting to drink that brand of beer again. I hid the other five bottles in the motor housing of a freezer at that hotel and later I told my Belgian friend in Simcoe about them. When he went to Belgium to visit his sister, he retrieved the bottles and thanked me very much for the beer.

~

When we returned to Canada I went back to

work and Erika went back to school. She registered in a full-time nursing program. She graduated and began work as a Registered Nurse. It was the best thing she could have ever done - next to marrying me. While she was in school I made myself useful. I did all the cooking, looked after the babies and pretty much everything else too. Erika had a job at our local hospital and a few years later she became a case manager in the community.

~

Meanwhile everything at JAX started to come apart at the seams for me. In fact things came to a screeching halt. While Jack Thornton – the owner was generous with my expense account he was frugal with my wages. I asked him for a raise and he refused it. What a shame. I did a lot of good work at that place and hated to leave. I thought I had secured a job for life there.

For years I had been the instructor at JAX, teaching new employees how to use measuring instruments; the purpose of specialized tools, fixtures and gauges. I taught the importance of safe working habits, the use of power equipment and high-speed machinery. Some of the people that came to work there had very little education and some didn't even know the multiplication table.

The biggest problem at JAX became the employee turnover. No sooner would a person learn the job and get good at it; he would quit and go to ABEX for higher wages. ABEX had remained in business after Jack Thornton left. The two were fierce competitors.

~

Andy Gunn, my best buddy, had one gigantic job to do. He was the plant superintendent in charge of all manufacturing activities, maintenance, scheduling and hiring. I don't believe there was a time when he ever met one schedule. None of it was his fault. Andy had seen many broken tire molds requiring immediate repair. Sometimes they would come in from a customer in the middle of the night. Often it was just a matter of someone having forgotten to take out an adjustable wrench or a socket and had closed the press on them. Too much emergency work took priority over regular jobs. I don't know how he was able to cope with those unbelievable tensions. I was continuously amazed with his coping then, and still am today. To top it all off, he was incredibly calm as if he was totally impervious to pressure.

I say this with a broken heart now, as I had to bid Andy goodbye on September 17, 2013. He left us on this side of the golf course that he loved so much. He left us thinking about him and wondering why – why did he have to leave so soon. No more golf games together in Myrtle Beach or at the Norfolk Golf and Country Club or anywhere else. Goodbye buddy. I'll miss you greatly. I have truly enjoyed your company.

~

ABEX was bent on putting JAX out of business but they never did succeed. Jack Thornton was a legend in his own time and in my book for sure. He lived for his customers. He was nine years older and actually died before Andy. I was very upset because no one had let me know about his passing. Even though we'd parted company I still thought a lot of him. He was always able to figure things out and with loyal employees like Andy and myself, things always worked out for him. It seemed like he was always on top of the world - in fact I believe he coined that phrase.

~

I once drove Jack to Decatur, Alabama in eleven hours! He had a new Chrysler and told me to drive it as fast as I could, he'd pay the fine if I was stopped for speeding. Fortunately we were never stopped even though I pushed that speedometre to two hundred and twenty kilometres an hour. I remember while driving through Cincinnati a person ahead of me suddenly slammed on the brakes and I had to brake too. Jack, sleeping in the back seat, crashed to the floor but was no worse for wear. He crawled back up onto the seat and went back to sleep. I grabbed a couple hamburgers on the way and we ate them on the run.

~

I don't know how much money JAX made or whether he made any money at all but he always got enough from his backers to build new plants. He had a shop in Brazil, one in Decatur, Alabama, one in Akron, Ohio and one in Oklahoma - maybe some other places as well. I drew up the plans for most of these shops.

Jack never really wanted to take time off work but when he did, he and his wife Bea would set sail in their little sailboat. He managed to go to places beyond my comprehension.

By the time I quit JAX I had made over ten thousand drawings. It broke my heart when I found out later that all my drawings had been destroyed. He burned them all. JAX eventually discontinued business in Simcoe and moved operations to the States.

It is a shame that he had to close the plant in Simcoe but he had no choice. JAX, like every other industry had stiff competition from third world countries. The shop union failed to recognize that fact and they decided to stick to their demands and two hundred people lost their jobs forever. JAX revenues were in excess of seven million dollars a year – a great loss to Simcoe, but devastating to all those employees.

Chapter Twenty-Four

Karoly-J Ltd. is born. I invent my Superlegs.

After I left JAX, I designed a Rain Tire and submitted it to B. F. Goodrich, Canada. I personally never got anywhere with it. Perhaps I was ahead of my time with the design? I will never know for sure.

I went to work for CML (Canners Machinery Limited) as the shop superintendent. It was a good move. My starting salary was at least a thousand dollars a month more than at JAX. I also received a bonus for any new customers I recruited for the company.

Originally CML catered to canning factories such as American Can and Del Monte. They had one salesman and he was busy with can-related orders. I persuaded several local industries such as Ontario Hydro, Texaco and Stelco to try our work and services. I started to develop a good relationship with these companies and my bonuses were fabulous - one to two thousand dollars extra per month. Those were the good old days.

~

We had some exciting projects going on at CML; and some good parties at my place where I used to put on a pretty interesting show with my magic tricks.

Being the PR person at my previous jobs I had a few gimmicks up my sleeve. I had good teachers too - my dad and Yany whom I idolized. Today a lot of the tricks they taught me have become common and I've forgotten most of them.

Even though CML had an efficient production line the writing was on the wall. After American Can, and Del Monte had ceased doing business in Simcoe, CML followed.

~

After I incorporated my company, Karoly-J Ltd., I rented a shop in Simcoe and started to manufacture

Super Legs. These were short stilts made of chrome plated metal. They had to be used in a special way - hands at the front and waist high. Out of the blue, Irwin Toys bought my entire inventory tooling and all. They were going to produce them themselves and I was to receive royalties. This deal looked pretty good. While I got paid for my product they never produced any *Super Legs.* I called Irwin Toys several times but got no answers. Since my production tools were gone I couldn't make any more stilts. I think they just wanted to get rid of a small-time competitor.

My *Super Legs* were cool enough though, that on September 8, 1979, they made the front page of the *Toronto Star* insert magazine. I even sold the few hundred that I had kept for myself.

~

It was time for a new job. Delhi Foundry was looking for a manager and they found one in me. Delhi Foundry and Farm Machinery was a prosperous well-managed company with several specialized products that catered mainly to the tobacco industry. While automatic leaf harvesting machines were on the market already most farmers still did their priming by hand. Priming tobacco means that only the ripe leaves are removed off the plant every day. I remember seeing hundreds of young people coming from Québec for the tobacco harvest. The pay was good and the job was relatively easy.

Norfolk County, Tillsonburg, Delhi, Simcoe, and Brantford generated billions of dollars from the 1950s until the tobacco quota buyout around 2007. There were more than thirty-seven hundred growers in the area at one time but only about six hundred were operating by 2013. In its heyday the *Tobacco Belt* supported a lot of the local economies and a great part of the fringe industries as well. I entered the mix on the tail end and put in my two cents worth for whatever good it created. But most importantly for me, I had fun.

I loved to work for Delhi Foundry. While there, I developed a wide variety of creative projects. Whenever there was a chance to make something easier to do, I would come up with an idea for a new machine. In my dreams at night I would visualize these machines working. Once you are an inventor you remain one for life and inventing occupies your dreams. I have to say, I take pride in my designs because they all worked and succeeded and most importantly, helped the farming industry.

Drawing and planning was something I did well. It's useful to have the ability to sketch an item before building it. Sometimes though, I didn't bother to make a diagram; simply put the machine together from suitable parts. I was good at my job - in fact I was so good that the owner of the foundry, Doug Cockburn gave me a free hand to do whatever I wanted.

Things got even more interesting when Doug expanded his operation to PEI - potato country. While the Foundry had been in business for a long time and was the lifeblood to the farmers in the Tobacco Belt, everyone could see the end of the tobacco industry was drawing near. Doug wanted to go out fighting. This suited me just fine.

This timing was the perfect opportunity for me to sink my teeth into some new work. I came up with a lot of useful equipment - the peanut processing machine for Picard Peanuts; the asparagus grader for growers; a travelling greenhouse watering system and more importantly the greenhouse tractor. I designed some state of the art greenhouses for tomato growers in Leamington, Ontario, as well. Some of these greenhouses were built around Simcoe too and that design became popular in the industry.

A ginseng washer was another one of my designs that became a very significant machine for that industry. Ginseng is dug out of the ground and has to be washed. Prior to my invention, the roots were cleaned in water either in a spring on the farm, or in a nearby creek. This was an unpleasant outside job, done by hand in the month of September. The most essential part of the ginseng harvesting process is to keep the roots as intact as possible. The ginseng washer took the washing operation indoors and it made a world of difference. That ginseng washer was an immediate success. The first customer at the Delhi Foundry was Gerald Nelson from Waterford and he was a very satisfied customer.

I am pleased to say I innovated on a potato harvesting machine, a pea harvester and land packer and also designed a greenhouse glass changer and strawberry de-capping machine and other items too numerous to mention. When I left the Foundry, those other items never materialized.

Although my innovative efforts helped a lot, they were sadly, not enough to save Delhi Foundry. New growing methods appeared on the horizon and a lot of production moved indoors- into greenhouses. Perhaps I could have carried on in the vegetable market but automation and the growing use of offshore labour took over. The rest is history.

~

In 1983, while still at Delhi Foundry I was watching the news one evening, when I heard an interesting story about a great Canadian man by the name of Lieutenant-Colonel Joseph Whiteside Boyle. He had been a legendary adventurer more widely known as 'Klondike Joe.' It wasn't easy to find literature about the man. Luckily I discovered a twenty-page pamphlet about this legend in the Delhi Library. I did more research on him and then composed a piece of music to honour him.

Once the song was ready I contacted the repatriation committee in Woodstock headed up by George Calder Q.C. When I sent him the song, he was thrilled and wanted to hear it sung. He commissioned a singer from the area, Woody Lambe.
I sent Woody the score and arranged a meeting with him at the Woodstock Town Hall where he performed my song to the committee. It was a success.

On June 29, 1983, at the Canada Day Celebrations, Klondike Joe Boyle's remains were reinterred in his hometown cemetery on Vansittart Avenue in Woodstock, Ontario, Canada. After the closing ceremonies in the Town Hall, Woody and I were introduced to the honoured guests. Woody, with his guitar, performed the song *Ode to Klondike Joe.* He received a standing ovation. This historical event was a momentous happening for both of us and an honour that few people will experience in their lifetime. I was covered in goose-bumps. Erika and the girls, and my in-laws were at the celebration cheering us on.

The local newspaper completed its write-up with the last stanza in my song...

"Travel fast, 'cause Canada is calling
Woodstock's where you rest in peace tonight."

From that day on, I couldn't stop writing poetry and composing songs.

~

My next interesting song was *Bicentario,* which I wrote for Ontario's Bicentennial celebration in 1984. It too was a success. I took my song to the Brant County School Board and they were thrilled. Along with the regional dignitaries I was invited to the celebration where several hundred school kids sang this song. What a wonderful experience.

I have written some Hungarian songs and poetry too, but I get more kicks out of writing in English, especially because my teacher almost failed me once in my own language - Hungarian. Despite having written and composed several songs I still don't play any instruments, and I can't read music. (*See songs and poetry in the epilogue*).

~

On April 26, 1986 on my way home from the States I heard some terrible news on my car radio - a nuclear plant meltdown had occurred in Chernobyl. The radiation fall out affected much of the European population. Many people died. Such was the fate of my six-year-old nephew Csaba, my sister's son. I had only met him once when he was about four years old. He was a beautiful little boy. He developed leukemia from the radiation fall-out. What a terrible tragedy it was.

My sister and her husband have visited us several times and we have shed many a tear over his death. They had two more children, both girls. Zita was born in 1985 and Boglarka in 1992. I know my sister and her husband will never recover from the loss of their beautiful little son. Attila, my brother and his wife Piroska also had a son Attila Jr., who was the same age as Csaba. Today he is married with a child of his own.

My brother Attila and his wife Piroska have a son Attila Jr. who has a child of his own as well.

~

After leaving Delhi Foundry in 1987 I tried a different line of work. I applied for and got a position as a marketing manager for a company called Ultramatic. This company did some fine screw-machining work and treated me exceptionally well. I visited a lot of customers in the United States and went to several industrial shows. One in Boston stands out in particular.

I stayed at the Back Bay Hilton in Boston where I ate grits with poached eggs and baked beans for breakfast. I had lobster at the legendary Union Oyster House and chowder at Pier #7. That was at the time when the *big dig* was taking place - everything in the city was under construction with detours everywhere. City driving was a real challenge. I can't tell you how many times I got lost or stuck on elevated highways and went around in circles until I finally found my way back to the hotel.

In December of the same year we went on a vacation to Florida and paid a visit to my aunt Theresa on Treasure Island. We used to stay at the Fargo Motel on Ocean Boulevard but the area has changed significantly. Gone are the small motels. They have been replaced by high rise hotels. I miss those little motels greatly. They used to be soooo cool! Things are changing a lot and life is moving very fast.

Chapter Twenty-five

I find a goldmine but it runs dry. I innovate on OLG's 649 draw tickets and get one free for my trouble. The ticket wasn't a winner. I write the book; Tusks of Terror. The publisher runs dry.

The constant travelling for Ultramatic finally got to me. When I saw an opportunity for a managerial position in Brantford, my favourite city, I grabbed it. I had a brief meeting with the LCS general manager Theo Biesma. The meeting took place at the Jolly Baron Inn where Erika and I had had our wedding reception. I offered to pay for lunch and Theo let me. After visiting the factory I made up my mind and took the job.

LCS was like Mr. Pup's belt buckle shop only one hundred times bigger. The plant made hydraulic hose fittings, crimpers and braided hose cutters for companies such as Gates Canada. This job turned out to be a good one for both LCS and me. A week or so, after they hired me, the innovating part of me went into full swing and the company started making more money.

Hydraulic fittings were made of leaded steel and we used a lot of that material. Around ten million dollar's worth a year. Suppliers were standing in line for LCS business. The fittings were made on screw machines. These machines were mechanical monsters and most had been built in the 1940s. Because more orders were coming in, I purchased some 'brand new' 1940 machines from a US army supply store and got rid of some prehistoric worn out equipment to make room for newer machinery and storage.

I had learned not to accept rush jobs because they only helped out negligent purchasing agents. It soon became apparent to me that certain parts were being ordered in small amounts and infrequently. It would be more profitable for the company to make three or four times the amount of those parts at the first order thereby saving money on costly future setups. A setup usually took six to eight hours. My idea of running extra parts worked out well and the left over parts were money in the bank.

With hundreds of different items to make and production so far behind, it took me three years just to catch up. I ordered materials well ahead of time and always insisted on adherence to delivery dates. It was an efficient shop.

~

Theo was an absentee manager. He came into the plant infrequently. Whenever he did show up, he would sit down at my desk and tell me funny stories about his recent trip to India. Occasionally he would repeat some of his favorite older stories. His wife's sister had married an Indian nobleman. Theo always called his wife, *The Wife*. Whenever he stayed until noon, he and I and the office manager Iris, would go out for lunch to any one of Brantford's best restaurants like the John Peel or Quan 99, a Vietnamese restaurant. Theo wasn't a technical person, but he should have been. His previous plant manager had taken him to the cleaners. That previous manager swiped enough machine parts and materials to build his own factory. It was almost the same size as LCS. Even after he left LCS, he tried to 'remove' some machine parts. His brother-in-law was still working at the plant. After I discovered some important tools missing, I figured out where they might have gone. I contacted the police and they suggested the company install some security cameras. We were just about to install them when someone saw the ex-manager's brother-in-law packing up an item and putting it in his toolbox. On his way out, I stopped him, retrieved the machine part and fired him right on the spot.

~

Even though the steel companies treated me as if I were a prince I never acted like Dennis had at ABEX or at JAX. I didn't eat raw steaks and didn't play ping pong all night but I did play a lot of golf; and on the best courses in the area. I also played some nice courses in New York State and Myrtle Beach. Along the way I dined at places unknown to most people. Those steel companies gave me that warm and cuddly loving feeling that my mother had given me when I was young.

However my cholesterol loved me too. It stuck to my arteries and almost did me in. My doctor told me I needed to eat the right food, drink no more than one alcoholic drink a day, exercise, and stop smoking! *Yeah, yeah, yeah.* I thought those warnings were for other people not me.

I was always ready with an excuse - mostly to myself. My favourite excuses were: I am European or; my father had high cholesterol or; alcohol never bothered me. By this time however, I had in fact quit smoking but I never told the doctor how old I had been when I started. In truth I had to quit smoking because I couldn't find any cigarettes, cigarillos, cigars, or pipe tobacco that could satisfy my yearning for nicotine. Before I quit, my days had started with a smoke and ended with a smoke. I smoked at least two packs of cigarettes a day, or several packs of cigarillos or cigars, or a pipe. I was hooked - big time! Despite my addiction I managed to quit cold turkey. It just took a lot of willpower.

My father had quit too. He started up again when he came to visit me in Canada in 1975. He loved Canadian cigarettes. He didn't die from smoking though. He died from the complications of an accident on April 13, 1983. After stepping down off a streetcar, he was hit by a vehicle. His death was unexpected; like Andy he left us too soon.

~

You can't stop progress. LCS and its ancient equipment and old concept of hydraulic fittings had had their day. New more sophisticated fittings came along which were made in third-world countries and were made on new machines with new manufacturing methods. The owner of LCS who was in his late eighties, threw in the towel. This is the way most small companies leave this world.

I wasn't ready to retire. I never wanted to retire. And I didn't. My mind was always active. Architecture always interested me and while watching television one day I was inspired by the Egyptian pyramids. The Friendship Festival was coming up and I thought this would be something interesting to have on display. I knew there were certain base dimensions, angles and

heights involved. I didn't want to reinvent the wheel; I just wanted to create something unique with my own dimensions and angles. I made a 'to scale' model and proceeded with preparations for the one I actually wanted to build named *'The Green Pavilion'*.

I made the sides using 6"X6" posts and standard 4'x8'plywood sheets. My idea was to have the materials undamaged and reusable, and I was looking for an artistic impact. When there was a light on at night inside this 'pavilion' the openings and the angles interacted and created very special effects. I was extremely pleased with the building and imagined a structure a hundred times larger than my model and thought the result would be breathtaking. I had wanted to get Carlos Ventin, the famous architect that rebuilt Canada's Parliament building in Ottawa excited about this project but he wasn't interested. Despite being turned down I advertised his company's name on my structure - free of charge.

I borrowed the materials from a local lumber yard and built my futuristic *Green Pavilion* for the Norfolk County Friendship Festival. It turned out rather interesting. A lot of people took photos of it and it was written up in the local newspaper. It did make people look and think which was the intent.

~

I am a gambling man and I bought a *Bingo* ticket every day for a year but the first prize always eluded me. One day I read a note on the back of the ticket which said that the first prize may have already been won. I considered this fraudulent, or at best, double talk. Why would anyone want to buy a ticket that had no first prize? So in 2004 I innovated on the *Bingo* ticket. Originally players would scratch numbers on the top portion of the ticket and would look for the matching number below but often would find no match. I wrote to the OLG and suggested to them that people would be happier if they always found a match, whether it was a winner or not. The lady responding for the OLG was very unfriendly and said she would send me a free ticket for my idea. To me that was a typical civil servant reaction. If it wasn't their idea, I could go to hell. She did send me a ticket and it wasn't a winner. I later discovered that they changed the format on the *Bingo* ticket to the one I had suggested. What a rip-off. I should have seen my lawyer first! Once an innovator, always an innovator – it is simply in my blood.

Chapter Twenty-Six

I invent YARDMARX/METERMARX - Golfcourse Fairway Distance Markers. What a great idea!

When I was younger and after I had learned how to hit a golf ball, I wanted to golf all the time. I was no Tiger Woods or Jack Nicklaus—if I had been, I wouldn't be writing this memoir, I'd be on a golf course somewhere, and someone else would be doing the writing! Early on, I had problems choosing the right club for the distance I needed to hit. Anyone that has ever handled golf clubs has surely noticed the numbers on them. Those numbers represent an intimate relationship between a club and the possible distance the ball can achieve with  that club. Generally speaking, the lowest number on a club would take the ball the furthest, providing it was hit properly.

I also couldn't estimate the distances on fairways. There are three permanent concrete markers on a fairway. Blue is for two hundred yards; white is for one hundred and fifty yards; and red is for one hundred yards. These markers are in the ground and cannot be moved. They represent the remaining distance to the centre of the green.

While out golfing, years after I had started, I noticed a piece of paper drifting in the wind. It had the numbers of the club written on it in one column, and the distance that club should yield in an opposite column. I carried that paper with me all the time as if it were the Bible. Half of my golfing dilemma was answered the other half wasn't. While I could see the number on the club I still didn't know how far I was from the centre of the green. I was rarely near any of those concrete distance markers; I was usually somewhere 'in-between'.

Needless to say, another idea hit me. Why not have more distance markers and have them more spread out? I solved the fairway distance problem with my markers which I named *YARDMARX/METERMARX* (in Europe they use meters instead of yards). My markers consisted of regular plastic golf cups (but used upside down). They would be embedded into the fairway with a regular golf cup sinker. They had advertising on them along with the distance to the centre of the green. Since my markers were more frequently spaced - twenty yards apart and six markers in a row - a golfer could always assess the distance to the centre of the green. The golf course would get the markers free and the advertisers got their message across to the public for a reasonable price. I dubbed it 'Ground level Communication'. Everyone agreed it was a win-win situation.

I had a website and my markers were selling nicely. Then a company in St. Louis, Missouri made me an offer. An offer I didn't think I should refuse. This time I was smart and didn't sign any papers until the deal was finalized. For almost a year documents were going back and forth until one day I phoned and there was no answer - the phone lines had been disconnected. The company had gone bankrupt.

I still own this marker business today, and I am ready to negotiate. This could be a lucrative business.

Chapter Twenty-Seven

I will always remember 2001.

In 2001, Erika and her father Rudy planned a six-week trip to Europe to visit the town of Tarutino where Rudy was born and which had become part of Ukraine. Their plane landed at Kiev Airport and they were shuttled to their hotel, the Royal Albert, in downtown Kiev. The date was September 11, 2001.

They were settling in and having a cup of coffee in the hotel restaurant when suddenly some patrons shot out of their seats and began shouting in Ukrainian and started running around in an alarming fashion. They were pointing at their cell phones and referring to television a lot, even though there was no television in the restaurant. Neither Erika nor Rudy understood what was happening but Erika knew there was a television in her room.   Perplexed, she took the elevator up to her room and turned on the television, tuning into CNN.

At that precise moment the news was showing a jet hitting one of the Twin Towers. At first Erika thought this was some kind of movie but when the commentator began to speak it became clear that the United States had been attacked and it was unclear as to what was going to happen next.

She rushed back down to her father trembling all the way and told him what she had seen and heard. At the time, Erika thought the Russians had attacked America and they would now have trouble getting back home. She cried. Rudy calmly said to her that he didn't believe it was the Russians - and he was right. Rudy knew some Ukrainian, just not enough to get a story right. Within a few days, though, everyone was aware of what had happened in New York.

This all occurred around 3:45 p.m. and the bank kiosk in the hotel would be closing at 4:00 p.m. A voice inside Erika's head told her to cash most of their American traveller's cheques because the possibility of a market crash was plausible. The kiosk teller was able to scrape together two thousand dollars' worth of rubles. Erika had made it just in time. The next four weeks of their trip was to be travelling around the Ukrainian region and as it turned out, for the following couple of weeks American traveller's cheques were essentially worthless in Ukraine. She had made a good call.

~

Rudy was originally from this area of Ukraine, but in his youth it had been a German district called Bessarabia, and everyone spoke German. When Erika and Rudy were ready to return home there was no direct flight from Kiev to Canada. They had to make a stopover in Vienna, Austria. By this time there were heavy restrictions put on what travellers could bring onboard. Items such as scissors, pocket knives and knitting needles were not allowed. After a gruelling luggage search they were ready to board a plane to Toronto. Erika had some manicure scissors confiscated by an exhausted and frustrated airport attendant, who was further aggravated when she asked him to get a wheelchair for Rudy. As the attendant wheeled Rudy into the airline waiting room, Erika began to cry. The stress of the luggage search, the attendant's rude behaviour and her worries for a safe flight home in these uncertain times had all become too much for her. What had happened to the world? To her greatest surprise, the attendant embraced her and assured her that the plane to Toronto had been security checked, not only once, but numerous times. They waited to board in saddened silence.

I paced for hours at Pearson International airport. It seemed the plane didn't arrive for an eternity. The *arrival* sign kept saying "delayed". No one was aware or could imagine how long and gruelling the pre-boarding 'search' had been for our friends and relatives. Erika and her father arrived, albeit three hours late, but all I cared about was that they were now safe.

Chapter Twenty-Eight

My neighbour plays golf in my back yard.

We had a cottage at Turkey Point, on Lake Erie and went there almost every weekend especially in the summer. Our daughters practically lived there. We had some very high phone bills. I wonder why.

My friend Keith Fletcher who was a little older than our girls, lived across Wamsley St. opposite my backyard. They all created their own amusement, not with explosives, but with benign things like golf balls. Keith asked me one day if they could hit golf balls across the street into my backyard. What a good idea I thought. Even I could practice some golf shots. Keith put a regular golf cup into the ground and put a flag into it. A hole in one or closest to the flag won that game.

One day a policeman in an unmarked vehicle was observing these cheerful young people traversing back and forth across the road with beer bottles in hand. To make a long story short, he gave two of the young men a ticket for consuming alcohol in a public place. That took the wind out of their fun. From there on they had to keep their eyes open.

~

I had municipal water at the cottage and it never dawned on me that the pipes might freeze in the winter. I drained the toilet, sink, and shower to prepare for winter and thought there was nothing else that could freeze. One day as I was talking to someone in the kitchen I heard water running. After the person left, I rechecked all the taps. They were all shut off. The only thing I could do was to remove some floor planks and look into the crawlspace under the building. I was shocked to see that water had almost completely filled the crawlspace! There were ripples on the water so I knew there was a break somewhere. I pondered for a few minutes over what to do next. Finally, I removed all my clothes and submerged myself into the cold water through a narrow gap in the floor. I felt around until I felt the source of the leak and to my surprise it wasn't what I had expected. which was a burst pipe. It was only a threaded pipe joint that had come apart. How that happened I'll never know. I reconnected the pipes by hand which stopped the leak and over time the water dissipated. The significance of this event is that it brought back memories of winter and freezing temperatures.

I had to immerse myself in icy water - naked. But the job had to be done and it got done. Had I not been inspecting the cottage that day, who knows what might have happened. Could the cottage have floated away? I know it would have cost me. For certain, I would have had an enormous water bill to pay. Surprisingly, I never even caught a cold.

But it did remind me of my younger days when I stood in line with holes in my shoes, freezing my toes off in a bread line.

The cottage is gone now, a next-door neighbour bought it and demolished it and extended his house onto the lot. He did a nice job.

~

My house on Oak Street in Simcoe is special to me because I designed an addition for it. I drew up the blue prints and added on a room for my pool table with a deck in the front and a deck in the back. Gord White my neighbour across the street welded the I-beams for the addition. Once I had the permits I hired a builder to erect the room and I finished the decks myself.

I proudly flew the Canadian flag from my new

deck. One night someone stole that flag. In retaliation I painted the Canadian flag onto my concrete driveway. "Steal this," I said after I finished painting it. This brought back memories of the communist signs I used to paint back in Hungary. While this flag story is one reason why my house is special to me, Gord's tales are no dogs either and they were special to him

~

When I was the manager at Delhi Foundry Gord used to come there often to purchase steel or have some materials shaped for him on our break press. Gord and I were very neighbourly. He used to tell me stories about his sons Ed and John, and sometimes he'd sit with me in my office and tell me about some of his customers.

Gord had a generator on his pickup which he used for welding and often, in the winter, to thaw out frozen water pipes. He said his arms always hurt him badly especially when he had to uncoil those generator cables and drag them into a house. Gord complained about his hurting arms a lot and swore marijuana eased his pain. I remember this because his problem was similar to mine.

One day Gord received a call from a woman whose water pipes had frozen. While weaving his cables through the basement rafters he knocked down several shoeboxes, spilling piles of hundred dollar bills all over the floor. Amazed, he picked them up and after he finished his work, he took the boxes upstairs and gave them to the woman. She thanked him very much and told him that she didn't know about the money because she had just bought the house through an estate sale a few months previous. Gord was speechless. That kind of story only happens in fairy tales. But there is more to Gord.

~

I was working in my front garden one day when I heard an explosion at Gord's house. Alarmed, I looked across the street and saw a small cloud of smoke and a round ring-like object rolling and bouncing off the curb in front of his house. It was the bottom of a steel barrel that he had been cutting in half to be used as a water trough. I went over to have a look and to make sure Gord was okay. He was holding his wrist and looking quite embarrassed. He said he had forgotten to sniff the barrel for fumes. I'd heard about such incidents before and suggested he fill the barrel with water before cutting it apart with a torch. He agreed. He said he was lucky that he had been standing to the side of the barrel when it exploded and not at the end that blew out.

~

I'd like to mention the most incredible man I've ever known. His name was Alex Hajdu, an almost impossible last name to pronounce in English. He was a Hungarian man. Alex lived at the lower end of Gunton Drive, on the same street as Gord.

Over the years I watched him ride his racing bike up the hill of Gunton Dr. Not a small task. Both Alex and his wife Anna, rode their bikes uphill - I used to push mine. They were a very athletic couple.

Alex and I actually became friends after meeting at Charles Jones' Industrial store in Nanticoke. He had finished university in Hungary and became a surveying engineer. He immigrated to Canada around 1965 with his wife and children. He contracted himself out and one of his jobs was to survey Stelco's rolling mills and locate them to a tolerance of one ten thousandth of an inch. This is a remarkable accomplishment anywhere in the world. This is almost like rocket science.

Sometimes Alex would ride his bike all the way to Stelco, which was about thirty kilometres from his house. He said that often on his way home he would get tired and would stop to rest. He would lay his bike into the ditch along St. John's Road, a very busy trucking highway, and would lie on his back and fall asleep. On one of those occasions someone reported a fatality and called for an ambulance. When the Ontario Provincial Police (OPP) and the ambulance arrived it sure looked like a fatality. However, Alex who was awakened by the siren noises, got up, moseyed over to his bike and prepared to ride away. Everyone was dumbfounded and didn't know what to say or do. This story was a little hard to believe but knowing Alex was an honest man, I had no doubts that it was true. He told me other stories just as bizarre if not more so. But that's for another book or two.

~

Alex always had some weird beer at his house that came in large cans. He liked to taste different brews. To be truthful, I hated his beers. I always drank *Molson Canadian* - about three swimming pools worth over my lifetime. Today I have maybe one beer a day. But beer brands aside, we became good friends.

Alex had only one problem - he never liked to finish anything. He started to build an elaborate deck, but never completed it. He started to redo his basement and again, never completed it. He took apart a BMW car, but never got it going. That car sat in his driveway for decades. Despite all this, I knew he was a brilliant man.

Alex loved my cooking. He wanted me to call him over whenever I made bean soup. That was his favourite.

Alex passed away in 2013. He gave me good advice on many things over the years - how to locate a property line, what to look for when buying a cordless drill and on and on. He also showed me a dust removal system he had designed and built for himself.

Miraculously, I too can ride my racer bike up that hill on Gunton Drive these days. I am in better shape now than I was about fifteen years ago.

Chapter Twenty-nine

My arthritis nearly kills me. Some dreams vanish.

I used to dread the nights and days when my arthritis was raging. By 2000 it had gotten really bad - I was in excruciating pain all the time. The pain became progressively worse. I underwent all kinds of tests and took powerful medications but nothing seemed to help. I started to think seriously about Gord and his conversation about marijuana helping with pain. But smoking isn't good for you, either!

It was at the point where I couldn't even allow my arms to hang down freely. I had to support one arm with the other. When I sat down I had to hold my arms at a ninety-degree angle to my body or rest them on a table. If I stood up I had to lean against a wall or a tree. In the evenings and into the night I would suffer in front of the TV and support my head on the blunt end of a fireplace poker as I moaned and cried. I kept murmuring, "Oh my God, oh my God," for hours on end, and thought about my poor mother and the hell she must have gone through with her arthritis until she died on December 10, 1972. During her time there was nothing other than Aspirin to ease pain but Aspirin didn't help my mom. I was taking Tylenol by the handful, and that didn't help either. Sometimes Erika would wake up in the middle of the night and ask me if she could help. I thanked her but there wasn't a damn thing anyone could do. I suffered almost a decade with this arthritic pain; the very worst of it being just before my carotid artery surgery.

My doctor finally sent me to a university

professor in London Ontario, who was a neurological specialist and even he couldn't help me. I could only sleep half an hour a night and consequently was totally exhausted during the day. I wondered how much longer this could go on. In order to keep my mind off the pain, I had to keep busy all the time. The minute I stopped being busy, the excruciating pain would be all I could think about. This pain felt like my arms were being pulled down by heavy weights and then set on fire.

In December of 2005 I was volunteering at the Panorama Welcoming Centre at the Junior Farmers building in Simcoe and selling my book *Tusks of Terror*, when a lady stopped at my book signing table. As I handed her one of my books she noticed the agony on my face and asked me if there was something wrong with my arm. I told her that my arthritis was killing me. She said she used to have the same problem and proceeded to tell me about a supplement that contained shark cartilage. She seemed like a very sincere person and I knew she was trying to help me - but shark cartilage? I thanked her very much and the next day, despite my misgivings I bought the supplement.

Within a week my pain had eased. Finally I could go to sleep. In less than a month I was feeling much better and another month later the pain was almost completely gone. I felt as though a miracle had happened! I wanted to kiss the angel who had stopped by my table, but I never saw her again.

The supplement worked for about three years and then insiduously, the pain began to creep back again. I wrote to the shark cartilage manufacturer but the company never replied. I was on my own again. My mom's pain came to mind once more - and the marijuana. This damn arthritis was going to kill me, I thought. But I wasn't ready to go!

~

After my book *Tusks of Terror* was published, I thought things looked pretty rosy. I sold close to five hundred copies in my hometown. RONA, Norfolk Office Supply, Roulston's and Picard Peanuts carried my book and I also marketed it at book fairs. The book's fictional story made it into the *Simcoe Reformer* and the *Brantford Expositor*. People called me in a panic asking if there actually were wild boars in the Norfolk County forest. I couldn't lie—I told them I didn't know however always reminded people that this was a *fiction*. I was counting on earning some money. I thought my book would sell well enough to make thousands of dollars and I could plan to see a specialist in the USA. My publisher mysteriously disappeared with my hopes and dreams of money. Back I went to square one. I had to put my innovating cap on again.

PAGE 10 / TIMES-REFORMER, TUESDAY, JULY 20, 2004

Arts & Entertainment

Norfolk has role in writer's new book

Chris Thomas
Times-Reformer

A veritable Renaissance man, Simcoe's Charles Jambor has added writing to his list of business and cultural pursuits.

Jambor has just had his first book published and his new address is "Cloud Nine."

"Tusks of Terror" is a simply told tale of wild boars running amok in the Norfolk County countryside often being released from pens by men vandals. The plot thickens when one of the scenes it family gored by the wild boars.

Jambor said the demise of the vandal was his literary retribution for acts of vandalism he's experienced.

"When I needed a villain, I was thinking about today's laws about young offenders and how they came all kinds of problems, yet never get punished," he told.

Wanting to write an adventure with a unique twist, Jambor drew upon a real life incident several years ago which occurred in the Delhi area.

A Hungarian farmer had imported some wild pigs to create a private hunting reserve. However, most of the pigs escaped and it took police and the Ministry of Natural Resources to round up the animals.

While the real life round-up went without incident, Jambor let his imagination loose.

The book is rife with familiar local place names and with a total of 41 characters, some people may even recognize themselves. Jambor confessed his protagonist is an embellishment of himself.

His book was born as a novella he started dabbling with back in 1974. After receiving encouragement from the late Brantford writer Donald Kerr Stanford, Jambor started dedicating more time to his literary work.

"It was all uphill from that point," he laughed.

Jambor soon discovered that writing was a daunting task, especially because English is not his native language.

"I don't know the language, spelling, and I wasn't educated here, yet I sat down and wrote a book," he said. "I think that's a hell of an accomplishment."

He readily admits the book is not for high brows.

"I wrote this for the ordinary lay person," Jambor said.

However, the hard part was getting the finished product published. But after an estimated 109 rejections, he found someone who opened the door to him.

Terry Williams of TreeSide Press, based in British Columbia, published the book after it came to him more than a year ago.

"Charles showed a lot of promise," Williams said. "He's such a dynamic guy, it was easy to work with him."

TreeSide Press devotes itself to promoting Canadian writers and authors and they have no shortage of submissions. He said they receive between 500 and 700 manuscripts each month. Less than one per cent are accepted for print.

Williams said the initial print run of Tusks of Terror was 3,000 copies. TreeSide Press has distribution arrangements with major booksellers in the United States, England and Australia. Catalogues are also sent to independent and chain book stores across Canada.

Jambor said he will be doing a number of local book signings, including one at the grand opening of the ROMA store in Simcoe on Sept. 11.

Chris Thomas
(519) 426-5710 ext. 135
e-mail cthomas@bowesnet.com

Chris Thomas/TIMES-REFORMER PHOTO
Simcoe's Charles Jambor has just recently had his first book of fiction published by TreeSide Press. He is currently working on two more books.

David Judd

MY FORUM

Pigs go hog wild in thriller novel

Charles Jambor has an active imagination. He has written Tusks of Terror, a rip-snorting, page-turning, novel about killer wild pigs on the loose in Norfolk County. Hard to believe it took more than 25 years for Jambor — or is that Ham-Boer — to find a publisher to bring home the bacon.

Here's what it says on the book's back cover:

It is comforting to know that there aren't any wild animals running loose in pristine Ontario communities.

What if there were? What if illegally kept wild boars were let loose by vandals? What if these dangerous animals belonged to a wealthy Hungarian farmer whose daughter is engaged to a game warden?

Will the game warden inform his office of this great danger, risking losing his fiancee? Or will he jeopardize his job by going along with his future father-in-law's bizarre plan? Will people know how to protect themselves from these unpredictable beasts? Can the wild boars be caught in time . . . before someone is hurt or even killed?"

Despite this compelling plot, scores of publishers turned down Tusks of Terror before it was recently picked up by TreeSide Press of

Tusks of Terror tells what might happen if wild boars escaped in Norfolk County.

Jambor doesn't claim Tusks of Terror is great literature. It's the kind of story you read in three hours on an airplane or while relaxing at the beach. Here's a sample of the dialogue at its ominous best:

"Are you coming hunting with us, Linda?" he asked.

"Where are you going hunting?" Linda asked and halted.

"In the forest. We're going after some wild pigs. They're as big as calves, I hear. You have to shoot 'em between the eyes, dead square. That's the only way to kill 'em."

"Come on, Andy, wild pigs aren't that big. Don't you know that?" she snickered and started walking again.

211

Chapter Thirty

I build 'my mansion on the hill' and it quickly becomes someone else's mansion.   .

In 2006 I purchased an old house on the corner of Prospect and Birch Streets in Port Dover. It was on a good-sized lot. I was planning to renovate it but there was just too much wrong with it. I decided to take the old house apart instead. I tried to save as much of the material as I could but even by pulling out all the nails I could only save some of the boards.

I subdivided the property and built a beautiful new house on the corner lot. I knew for sure that when I finished my house it was one hundred percent correct in all respects.

My building project rolled along nicely but unfortunately at the time when it was half done in 2008, the bottom fell out of the economy greatly affecting the sales of upper end real estate. My million dollar *mansion on the hill* ratcheted down a few hundred thousand dollars in value and stood there empty for some time. One day I read about a savvy real estate lady, named Cindy Pichette of Bauer Realty Inc. and fortunately within a few months the property was sold. My arms were still aching; not as bad as before and I still couldn't sleep at night.

~

Around this same time after enjoying some sun-tanning on my deck and heading back into my house, I suddenly experienced a dizzy spell. It only lasted for two seconds, but I certainly noticed it. At the time I believed it to be a precursor of something more sinister; a warning. That warning became reality about fourteen months later in a big way.

I was calmly shaving one morning and had a stroke. Erika immediately rushed me to the Norfolk General Hospital. I was transported to the stroke unit in Brantford for some tests. The doctors found that my carotid arteries were badly obstructed. An appointment was arranged for surgery. This time I thought, I was going to kick the bucket for sure. But, I still wasn't ready - and I'm still not today. I had checked with other people who had undergone a similar surgery and they all cheered me on telling me not to worry. Even my buddy Andy Gunn (now deceased), who had undergone bypass surgery, told me not to fear anything.

The surgery was scheduled at the Juravinski Hospital in Hamilton for October 25, 2010, at 11 a.m. I was lying on a gurney waiting for the operation to proceed but it didn't. At 4 p.m. they cancelled my surgery. I died a thousand deaths on that gurney. The surgery was rescheduled for December 9, 2010, and was a success. Much to my delight I lived, and my arms don't hurt anymore - not at all!

No doctor would tell me with any certainty why my arms were not hurting any more. I made the assumption that the reason my arthritic pain was gone, was because my arteries had been cleared thereby improving blood circulation. Who knows.

~

After my surgery as I was coming out of the anesthetic I heard some people talking on the other side of the vinyl room divider. One of them sounded familiar. He sounded like the man whose wife sold corn by the highway near my home. This was surely impossible. What! Another *Fred* incident? What in the world would this man be doing in this Hamilton hospital? He certainly hadn't come to see me because he didn't know I was in here.

The longer I listened to the conversation the more convinced I became that it was someone I knew. After the nurse unhooked me from the wires and hoses she told me I could go home. I was delighted.

While waiting for Erika to pick me up I dozed off. When she arrived I got dressed and headed over to the ward next door. And there he was, Walter, my buddy from the highway corn stand in Simcoe. He'd had a bad accident. He'd fallen onto a metal railing and fractured his arm. Walter had to have emergency surgery otherwise he could have lost that arm. He was conscious but still heavily drugged. He couldn't believe seeing me there and I told him I felt the same way. He was so ecstatic to see me that he had tears in his eyes. Caught up in his emotions, I almost cried, too. In hindsight, I think it was all the painkillers we were on...

Several months later I visited him at his house and we had a beer. He was back to work but his arm was still hurting. He told me he would be okay and I was sure he would be.

Chapter Thirty-One

I revel in the 'Friday the Thirteenth' motor bike meets. For the first time since 1955, I see a Moto Guzzi.

Every Friday the 13th a *world-class event* comes to Port Dover, Ontario, Canada. Thousands of bikers from all over the continent converge on the town for a day of friendship and celebration. The only event that I know of that is bigger than this is the one in Daytona Beach, Florida, and that lasts for a week. Several hundred thousand bikers go to that meet because the venue is much larger than Port Dover. It would be impossible to host a hundred thousand bikers in Port Dover, a town of six thousand. I have been going to the 'Dover' events since July 1984 and I wish I could have been part of its inception back in November of 1981.

Rain or shine, summer or winter, the bikers roar into Port Dover and people cover every square foot of the downtown. One famous person who wears nothing but a thong summer or winter, makes his run down Main Street at every event. He is affectionately referred to as Paul the "Thong Man". He only makes one run when it's freezing cold. In the summer he parades around all afternoon and poses for photographs - free of charge.

Other than having a few bottles of brew, most bikers come for the camaraderie and to say hello to old friends and to make new ones. The Hell's Angels come too and contrary to popular belief they don't create problems.

My American cousins come to this event whenever possible. It is always a pleasure to see them because they are great people and a lot of fun.

I have seen every kind of motorbike imaginable

represented at this event, even one with a casket for a side car. I was thrilled when I saw my favourite bike, the Moto Guzzi. That brought back a flood of great memories for me.

~

My main hobby used to be gardening. Now it is writing. This is a new part of my life and the beginning of an exciting and satisfying era. I have always had a sense of accomplishment but it is different today; today I have arrived.

My schooling served me well and provided me with a solid foundation; something I could build on. Now I am finally doing what I truly enjoy - telling stories. My vivid imagination is full of tales.

My next book is called; *'The Passengers'*. A trusted critique of mine Bernard Crawshaw, put it this way: *"What can authorities do if people are abducted and there is no ransom demand? While the story starts with a mystery, it ends with an unexpected surprise"*.

I am in the process now of writing another book called: *'Fire in the gut'*. This story scares even me and I am the writer.

~

Finally, I will be forever grateful to Canada. It has provided me with the opportunity to have a family and follow my dreams. To those who immigrate here, I have this to say: Canada is the best and the most amazing country in the whole world. It truly is *My Promised Land.*

I am thankful for the opportunity of being able to tell my lifetime story.

When anyone asks me how I am doing, my forever response is "Top of the world!"

Charles Eric Jambor

Picture Gallery

Family and Friends

Inventions

Poetry and Songs

Left to right – old family portraits: my father is the baby; my mother; my father; my sister Aniko, Erika & my parents; my mother at a young age; my sister and her fiancé; my sister's wedding picture.

Our daughters – Bobbi & Carrie

My poker buddies

Some of the Yambor family: Alex Jr., Erika, Rocky, Diana, Johnny Bull, Uncle Alex.

The Yambor (and a Jambor):
Diana, Jackie
Erika, Betty, Alex Jr. & Rocky.

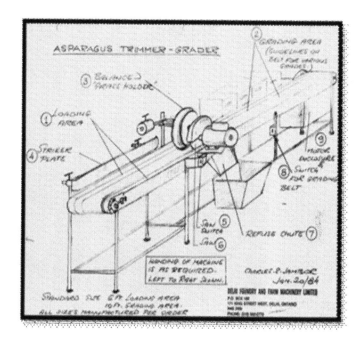

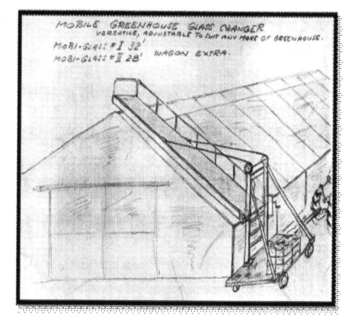

Charles Eric Jambor

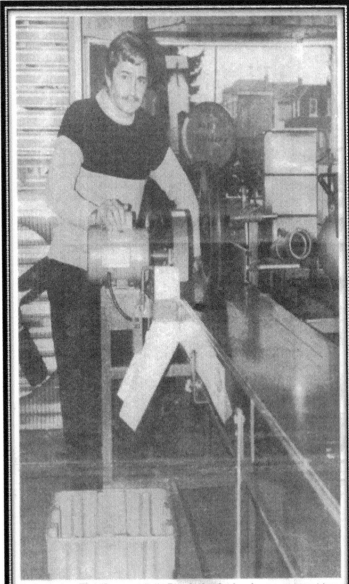

Charles Jambor, Plant Manager at Delhi Foundry has developed a new asparagus trimmer and grader that could increase efficiency and reduce labour costs by up to 50 per cent. It is available at Delhi Foundry now and can be custom built. (Staff Photo)

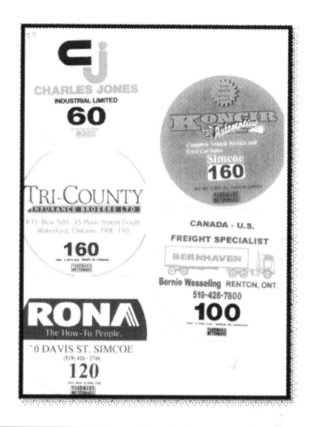

The Ginseng Washer

BOYLE REMEMBERED WITH SONG — Charles E. Jambor of Simcoe wrote Ode to Klondike Joe which was sung in Woodstock at the re-burial ceremony of Joe Boyle, a unique Canadian-born hero figure who has until recently been forgotten in Canada. (Staff Photo)

Budding Simcoe songwriter
pens 'Ode to Klondike Joe'

By ROSE SIMONE
Staff Writer

Because of Charles Jambor of Simcoe, Joe Boyle may become more than the "Joe Who?" of Canadian History.

Jambor, who has no professional musical background, has written and composed a song about the Canadian hero, Joe Boyle, whose name is better known in Europe than in Canada.

Boyle died and was buried in England in 1923, but after 7½ years of effort his remains were brought back to Woodstock and buried there in a military ceremony last Wednesday.

Boyle is better known as "Klondike Joe" who spent his early years in Woodstock and became rich in the Yukon gold rush.

He set up, financed and equipped a 50-man machine gun unit in the First World War. He acted as a consultant to the Russian government to straighten out that country's railway problems which prevented food from moving as people were dying of starvation.

In Romania, Boyle maneuvered a train through fighting Bolshevick forces and carried that country's jewels and treasury notes to safety. He was decorated by Queen Marie of Romania with whom he developed a beautiful friendship.

Jambor said he first heard about Boyle on a newscast, which spoke of Boyle's remains being brought back to Canada. That inspired him to write his song "Ode to Klondike Joe" which was sung by Woody Lamb of Woodstock during Boyle's re-burial ceremony last Wednesday.

Jambor said he's been in Canada for 27 years (he is from Hungary) and that in that time, this is the first Canadian hero that he's heard much about.

He went to the Delhi Library and took out a biography about Joe Boyle to help him write the words to the song.

Jambor cannot read music but he bought his children an organ that he likes to compose tunes on. By writing the letters down as he played, he put together "Ode to Klondike Joe."

He tried to get his song accepted by various sources but he reached the organizers of the committee to bring back Joe Boyle.

He sent the song to Woodstock and "they accepted it."

This success has encouraged Jambor to go on with his song writing.

He seems to have a natural talent for it and says he turns out the songs very quickly. He says he plays out the tune in his head. The Ode to Klondike Joe only took three hours to write, said Jambor.

He says he likes "simple, catchy tunes."

Jambor is happy that he has found an artistic endeavour he can enjoy some success at. He said he's tried writing a book, sketching and other art forms but those have never sold or gone anywhere.

It's his hope that the song "Ode to Klondike Joe" gets published and that perhaps it will be passed down as a song from the past causing Joe Boyle to be remembered as a Canadian hero in the years to come.

Poetry and Songs

by
Charles Eric Jambor

ONTARIO
(my 'Promised Land')

Rivers sparkled; the grass was green
The place was Canada
They disembarked the Loyalists
In Nova Scotia
They gave them food, and they gave them tools
And they gave them seeds to sow
On a track of land between the lakes
Called Ontario

Ontario, Ontario, Ontario, Ontario

Trees were tall; the game was fair
The land was rich as gold
They worked, they played, they fought their wars
They weathered bitter cold
They made peace with the Indians
Who shared with them the land
They made peace with the Lord above
Who guided their hand

Hey Seneca, hey Oneida, hey Iroquois, hey Cayuga

Skies were blue and lakes were clear
Their will was hard as steel
They invited the immigrants
And they invited the skilled
They honoured Brant; they honoured Bell
They honoured Pauline
They loved the Cats; they loved the Leafs
And they loved to see them win

Go Ottawa, go Moosonee, go Niagara, go Sudbury

Rivers sparkle, the grass is green
The land is rich as gold
The trees are tall, and the game is fair
And the ideas are bold
Skies are blue, and the air is clean
And there's still a place to grow
On the track of land between the lakes
Called Ontario
Ontario, Ontario, Ontario, Ontario

ODE TO KLONDIKE JOE 1867 – 1923
*(This song was performed by Woody Lambe at the
Repatriation Ceremonies of Klondike Joe Boyle's
remains to Woodstock, Ontario, June 29, 1983.)*

Summer's coming; days are getting warmer
Streams are calm; you'll make it to the Yukon

Travel fast 'cause Klondike Valley wants you
Dawson City waits for you tonight
Dawson City waits for you tonight

Smoky beer halls, saloon, Monte Carlo
Eldorado's nuggets made you rich

Travel fast 'cause Swiftwater Bill wants you
San Francisco is where you'll sleep tonight
San Francisco is where you'll sleep tonight

They call you Joe; they call you King of Klondike
They work your dredges, railroads and your mines

Travel fast 'cause Oxford County wants you
"The Firs' is where your mother is tonight
"The Firs' is where your mother is tonight

Clouds are turning black, and there is thunder
Or is that the bellowing of guns

Travel fast 'cause Romania wants you
Europe is craving blood-letting tonight
Europe is craving blood-letting tonight

London, Bergen, Moscow, and in Jassy
Earned your stars like no one has before

Travel fast 'cause Canada is calling
Woodstock is where you'll rest in peace tonight

Travel fast 'cause Klondike Valley wants you
Dawson City waits for you tonight
Woodstock is where you'll rest in peace tonight
Woodstock is where you'll rest in peace tonight

POET'S CORNER

MY BEAUTIFUL BRIDE
(a plea to end the madness)

To my brother in Yugoslavia
It is quiet now
Only a young man in camouflage cries softly
As he kneels beside a broken body
Of a woman in her teens—perhaps nineteen
Her clothes are torn
Her right breast exposed
Pink panties
He's never seen her like this before
Now he sees her like this … when she is dead

He's never touched her breast before
She didn't let him
He now does, a breast soaked in tears
Her breast is firm
But cold … cold as ice

She looks
She has a permissive look in her eyes…
Go ahead, brother, touch her
Fondle her—now, she doesn't mind

Her father won't object; he too is dead
Her mother would though, but she's in pieces
All over in the yard in front of a
Demolished house that was built two hundred years ago
Beneath a broken pear tree
That took a lifetime to grow
Next to a garden full of tomatoes
Onions
Cucumbers
Potatoes—ready to pick

Milan—my brother cries
I cry as I write!
Because I understand that
All this talk about
Disarmament
Conservation
Recycling
Emission control
Animal rights are a crock of
BULLSHIT!
Where's Greenpeace now
Where's Suzuki
Where's Nader
Where's the Pope
The Human Rights Activist
George Bush
Billy Graham
Brian Mulroney, Mila … Mila?

Where is the billion dollar
United Nations
The toothless lion
Lion?
An opossum is more like it

Milan cries another tear
Somebody's done him wrong
He silently vows to get even
He wipes the tears from his face
He spins the tires on a Toyota pickup
As he drives away
Up the hill—near his old school camp
The wedding's off—obviously.

WELCOME TO THE TENTH ANNUAL TOWN
LEVEE
SUNDAY, JANUARY 8, 1994 - SIMCOE TOWN
HALL

SIMCOE PRETTY

Sun is shining, a new day in our town
In Lynnwood Park, the Friendship Fest is on
Streets are full of gaiety
Art and craft activity
Celebrating Simcoe's Legacy
(Refrain)
You sensed our will some 200 years ago
You've trusted us, we'd flourish, we'd grow
John Graves Simcoe, 200 years ago

Guitars strumming, fun days in our town
Bells are ringing, Tower Carillon
Streets are full of gaiety
Tug-of-war activity
Celebrating Simcoe's legacy
(Refrain)
Shops are busy; farms are in demand
Prosperity describes our land

Parks are full of gaiety
Ducks and Fair activity
Celebrating Simcoe's legacy
(Refrain)
Snow is falling; it's winter in our town
Panorama, beauty all around
Streets are full of gaiety
Christmas lights and fantasy
Simcoe is where I always want to be
You sensed our will some 200 years ago
You've trusted us, we'd flourish, we'd grow
John Graves Simcoe, Canada, Ontario

TO MY BROTHER IN YUGOSLAVIA
(a letter to a fictional brother)

By the time the white lilacs turned to rust
I thought you would have come to your senses
But you haven't

Remember, you always liked to smell the lilacs in our
back yard

Remember, Mom used to say
"He who likes flowers can't be bad"

So why are you bad?

Why are you shooting children, women, old folks
Someone's girlfriend (like the way somebody shot
yours.)

Have you lost your mind?

When you come to Canada, as I hope you will,
You'll see how we get along here

But when you come, brother
Leave your history book at home
Better still burn all your history books NOW!

And perhaps
By the time the white lilacs turn to rust again
I'll see you back "home" and we'll vacation
By the Adriatic sea in Rijeka

THE GHOST WRITER

Sitting at the Station
Waiting for the Greyhound
Trying very hard to write a country song
The melody eludes me
Lyrics don't come easy
But a friend beside me tells me don't give up
He says: write about your daughter
Father and dear old mother
Why not write about your wife in Tennessee
Write about the lonely
The girl whose heart is broken
Or the sinner man with handcuffs on his hands

Write a song of love
Or of the Lord above
Or of the blues in St. Louis
Write a song of fame
Or of the man whose name
Will go down in history

And he says: write about the good times
Write about the bad times
Why not write a song of life and liberty
So I wrote about the story
That unfolded before me
'Cause the tale was here for a hundred country songs

Write a song of joy
Or of the men at war
Or of the hills of Kentucky

Write a song of faith
Or of the will that made
This land of ours the land of the free

Standing in the lobby
Of good old Grand Ole Opry
All these famous people want to shake my hand
But the friend who stands beside me
Deserves all the glory
Because he's the one who wrote this country song

He's the one with the words
He's the one with the tune
He's the one who writes the songs

He's the one who thinks
He's the one who knows
He's one who wrote this country song
He's the one with the words
He's the one with the tune
He's the one who writes the songs

He's the one who thinks
He's the one who knows

He's the one who wrote this country song

POLKADOT REINDEER

Cheery chin cheer
Christmas is here
Better be good tonight

Cheery chin cheer
Put on your jammies
Hurry turn off the light

Cheery chin cheer
Sleigh bells are ringing
Santa is on his way

Cheery chin cheer
When he gets here
Hope we can make him stay

Bright and shine moonlit night
Amazing things are happening
Instead of Rudolph from the sky
Polka dot reindeer descending

Cheery chin cheer
Says the first deer
My name is Speckle Dot

Cheery chin cheer
Poko is here
Second in this happy lot

Cheery chin cheer

Dotty reindeer
I am the third to trot

Cheery chin cheer
Funniest deer
His name is Polka Dot

Puffy white bags are full of toys
Santa can hardly move them
Dotty and Poko give a hand
Polka dot will divide them

Cheery chin cheer
Have a good year
Play with your toys a lot

Cheery chin cheer
Remember dear
We are a happy lot

Cheery chin cheer
Polka dot deer
That's what we like to be
Cheery chin cheer
It's nice to be here
In polka dot fantasy

THE PLAGUE AND THE GUN

In the year of thirteen fifty-one
A sailor dies—the Black Death had just begun   (hum)
The Black Death had just begun

Chorus: The Black Death had just begun

In the year of thirteen fifty-three
Europe cries and forfeits every three
Lose the weak and strong
Bury old and young

Chorus: Bury old and young

In the year of thirteen fifty-five
Dr. Smith and Dr. Black survive
They devise a cure
The plague no longer rules

Chorus: The plague no longer rules

In the year of nineteen eighty-one
A young man dies—and AIDS had just begun   (hum)
And AIDS had just begun

Chorus: And AIDS had just begun

In the year of nineteen ninety-three
L.A. cries and buries every three
They bury weak and strong
Father and his son
Chorus: Father and his son
In the year of nineteen ninety-nine
All is quiet, and everyone has died   (hum)
The plague has finally won
AIDS has beat the gun
AIDS has beat the Colt Forty-Five gun

Chorus: AIDS has beat the Colt Forty-Five gun

SONG OF THE "NEW" EXILES

You raised your lamp beside the golden door
You saved the hope, the shelter for the poor
Your mother tongue is Liberty
Your breath is opportunity
You teach your children how to be free

They came to you a hundred years ago
You promised them you'd never let them go
My forefathers a hundred years ago

Thunder roared, and tremors shook the land
The guiding lamp light quivered in your hand
Your heart was full of agony
You foresaw their destiny
Yet you dried your eyes and sent your sons to war

They came to you a hundred years ago
You promised them you'd never let them go
My foremothers a hundred years ago

When April came your gown had a tear
Your Crown was drab, your shoe needed repair
You called upon your family
They came to keep you company
Your sons came back to decorate your hair

They came to you a hundred years ago
You promised them you'd never let them go
My fore-brothers a hundred years ago

Bless the torch, you hold up to the sky
Bless the land, our "Mother of the Exiles"
You gave us love and dignity
Raised us to maturity

You taught your children to be free

We came to you a hundred years ago
You kept your promise, you didn't let us go
Our brothers still have a century to go
Our sisters still have a century to go
...a century to go
...a century to go

FIRST IN MY HEART...

First in my heart
You were the first in my heart
Tearing me apart
You were tearing me apart from the start
First in my heart
I love you with all of my heart!

First in my heart, why do you treat me this way
Why do you hurt, why do you tear me apart
First in my heart
I love you with all of my heart

First in my heart
You were the first in my heart
Breaking my heart
You were breaking my heart from the start
First in my heart
I love you with all of my heart!

First in my heart, why do you promise to stay
Why do you lie, why do you treat me this way

First in my heart
I love you with all of my heart!

First in my heart
You were first in my heart
Tearing me apart
You were tearing me apart from the start
First in my heart
I love you with all of my heart!

I love you with all of my heart!
I love you with all of my heart!

THE GOLD BRICK HOTEL

Loneliness Street in Forget-me town
Third floor in Gold Brick Hotel
Night after night, Gail sits by the door
But no one is ringing her bell

She already has her make-up on
She anxiously stares at the door
She puts down her bible and fixes her hair
She looks in the mirror and prays: God…
Please, someone come to my door
Please, someone come to my door

Loneliness Street in Forget-me town
Third floor in Gold Brick Hotel
It's Saturday night, and it's five after nine
And someone is ringing her bell

She already has her make-up on
She nervously looks at the door

She takes a few steps, and she asks "Who is it?"
She waits and a deep voice speaks: "Mona…?"
With tears in her eyes, she says: "No."
With tears in her eyes, she says; "No."

Loneliness Street in Forget-me town
Third floor in Gold Brick Hotel
It's Saturday night, and she is five after sixty
And no one is ringing her bell

Forever she has her make-up on
Her eyes are still fixed on the door
Her bible is tattered, and her hair is white
She still looks in the mirror and prays; God…
Please, someone come to my door
Please, someone come to my door

TO MY PUPPY, MY EVER LASTING LOVE

Having you here beside me
Petting your angel face
Feeling your warm little body
Nothing can take your place

You're my morning sunshine
You are my daily joy
You're in my evening prayer
You are the one I adore.

Want you to know
I love you so
When you are here
Heaven is near

Holding you in my arms dear
Stroking your velvet hair
Feeling your warm little heartbeat
Such wonderful times we share

You brightened up my life, pup
You let me recognize
The beauty and affection
Gentleness in your eyes
(Refrain)
Keeping you here beside me
Cuddling your darling face
Feeling your warm little body
Nothing can take your place

You are my greatest pleasure
My little puppy dog
The jewel of creation
My everlasting love
(Refrain)
(Refrain)

BALLAD OF STU AND LILLIAN KELLY AND THE FOURTEEN MILLION BUCKS

My favourite draw is six-forty-nine
Richer than Lottario
As for the odds to win the jackpot
Don't tell me, I don't want to know

Don't tell me I don't want to know

Driving my rig on route twenty-four
My mind is on sweet Lillian

Hugging the shoulder around the bend
Don't tell me this is the end

Don't tell me this is the end

Watching the news on channel thirteen
Reality enters my mind
The numbers I picked, the numbers came up
On Saturday's six-forty-nine

On Saturday's six-forty-nine

Goodbye to Finch and goodbye to Queen
Goodbye to Thibodeau
Goodbye to friends on route twenty-four
Goodbye we won all the dough

Goodbye we won all the dough

My favourite draw is six-forty-nine
The big one I'll never forget
Winning the money was easy to do
Spending it will be the task

Spending it will be the task.

ONE FINAL NOTE

For those of us who escaped from a war-torn country,
from oppression and destitution, and settled in
North America, it was a joy. Millions of people can
only dream of freedom, education, prosperity and
happiness in a free world. It is Shangri-La.
Some got lucky. I became one of them.

Made in the USA
Charleston, SC
10 April 2015